CONCILIUM

concilium 1994/4

MYSTICISM AND THE INSTITUTIONAL CRISIS

Edited by

Christian Duquoc and
Gustavo Gutiérrez

SCM Press · London
Orbis Books · Maryknoll

Published by SCM Press Ltd, 26–30 Tottenham Road, London N1
and by Orbis Books, Maryknoll, NY 10545

ISBN: 0 334 03027 7 (UK)
ISBN: 0 88344 879 3 (USA)

Typeset at The Spartan Press Ltd, Lymington, Hants
Printed by Mackays of Chatham, Kent

Concilium: Published February, April, June, August, October, December.

Contents

Introduction: Mysticism and the Institutional Church

The preparation of this issue on spirituality has been marked by mourning: Sebastian Kappen died on 1 December 1993 at Bangalore, having just finished (on 29 November) the article that we are publishing in it. The editorial directors and committee of the Spirituality section of *Concilium* offer his family and friends their deep condolences. His work in search of a Hindu form of Christian expression and practice, his fight against all forms of the idolatry of power and money which led him to explore the possibilities of Marxism as originally conceived, and betrayed by its Soviet form, explain his personal involvement in the article published here. One of his colleagues asked the editorial directors not to correct the structure and content of the article in any way. This request clearly indicated that if we disagreed with certain points of his work we were not to publish it; we were to respect it as a whole. This article represents Kappen's testament: one does not correct a testament after the death of the testator. It can be read as it was written. We are aware that some readers will find the judgments made on the West too severe, or what is said in it about Asian religions too indulgent. But even if they do not share the opinion which is expressed, we hope that they will consider what lies behind so free a piece of writing. Its very excesses, if there are any, prompt more thought than would a balanced piece which aimed not to offend the varied public for this journal. These excesses express the suffering which has been caused by an encounter that has turned into cultural and religious imperialism. The alternative proposed opens up perspectives which are misunderstood in the West. The christocentric unilateralism which reigns there leads to a forgetfulness of the legitimacy of other experiences: if the form of mysticism envisaged in this article is unfamiliar to us, it will be all the more fruitful for our excessively narrow understanding of Christianity and our excessively institutional practice.

What in fact is this issue about? It is about what is beyond question a very old debate in Christianity between the safe course proposed by the institution and the mystical adventure outside the marked tracks. The articles which comprise it do not so much summarize the recurrent debate as show what is always at stake in this tension. What is at stake always involves suffering and a question. Suffering: often as a church we do not know how to listen, we teach dead truths, we get hung up on the pure objectivity of what is said, and take no interest in the destiny of the individual, thinking only in terms of the collective interest. Where that happens the individual is isolated and enslaved to his or her God. It is this practice which is plunging the institutional church into crisis.

A question: if institutional intermediaries fail, is it not necessary to turn away from the God that they impose on us and without going through the church approach the God of Jesus who is presented as the God of the living? In short, is it not necessary, if we are to find a way to God, to take a route which is close to mystical experience? Many people think so, for example Drewermann.

In fact, the truth of the God of mysticism comes from the depths of human beings: it is not conveyed by the cold objectivity of institutional teaching, but breaks out in immediate contact with God; that is the reason why it gives an absolute priority to the individual, taking up a great many experiences. In this truth, which is both existential and mystical, we ourselves are always the concern. It also liberates, since there is no way to God which is not a way towards one's own flourishing.

Here we meet up with the conclusions of our consultations with the Editorial Committee of the section on Spirituality: they can be summed up like this.

'At present there is great curiosity about mysticism; it is inversely proportional to the allergy provoked by the ecclesiastical institutions. Many people feel that these institutions have fallen into disuse because of their failure to respond to the spiritual hunger which marks the end of our century. This desire seeks immediacy with God. In this perspective, many people think that as a result of their dogmatic or practical intransigence the churches are a source of violence and do not encourage spiritual experience. In any case, if all are agreed that the ecclesiastical institutions are in crisis, few explain the interest in mysticism by the recession in the churches. What we have here is rather an application to the experience of the divine of a general refusal to accept control. God can only be encountered where one lives in freedom.'

We believe that a pluralist approach to this question will be of interest. So no single theory about the interest in mysticism and the rejection of institutions is proposed here. The aim of the issue is to analyse the forms of experience of God which stand apart from common institutional experience, without necessarily opposing them to that experience or rejecting institutional control. Indeed it seems that an infatuation with mysticism risks underestimating what is at stake and tends to make a God without definite features equivalent to the God of Jesus, the God to whom Jesus has given a face and to whom the institutions of the church claim to bear faithful witness.

The church's institutions draw their force from the scripture on which they lean, but they manifest the inherent weakness of a word which is too involved in the human dimension. The God of mysticism, as Drewermann imagines him, captivates by the silence which is the form of his proximity. This silence is peopled with our words which aim at expressing the ineffable without ever possessing it. The impact of the words of the Bible, in a historical context and reinterpreted by the church, seem to put a spell on the spiritual creativity of the subject; the words of the Bible are presented more as a law than as the call to a dialogue. The human subject is compelled to obey, is not stimulated as a conversation partner. Is it so certain that the God of mysticism who, though silent, is present, is nearer than the God who speaks, albeit in human forms? Is it so certain that, even in the form of a prohibition, the word does not do more to structure the approach to God, than the retreat of the divine into ineffable sound? We leave the question open, hoping that the contributions here, with their different approaches and sometimes opposed in their perspectives, will allow readers to see the basic questions which arise out of the diversity of spiritual experiences.

We must return to this distancing: it is neither arbitrary nor fantasy. In the article which opens this issue and which he has entitled 'The Christian Rule of Mystical Experience', Yves Cattin freely confronts the paradox to which it leads:

'Experience proves both ineffable and incontestable. It knows that it is put in question, but it is vowed to silence. If this experience undertakes to speak of the God who visits it, it appeals, at the very heart of the most profound subjectivity, to a truth and an objectivity which are those of God himself . . . It has to confront the otherness of the word of God and the way in which it is brought to bear in the community of believers.'

The author establishes that one cannot escape from this paradox at the expense of one of the poles. But the otherness of the common Word remains the rule, since it alone guarantees that the mystical experience is not an idolatry of the self but a departure from the self in the direction of the God who comes.

This places the discussion firmly in context. Carlo Carozzo goes on to relate mysticism to the modern appetite for access to the divine. He discerns in this appetite an experience of the world and the self as an expression of the divine. The features of the divine are barely defined; it is silence. But the request for an almost maternal presence can be perceived in what he writes. By its objectivity and its authoritarian character, the institution does not honour this demand. It is afraid of it. It also has to rediscover in the faith that it proclaims a status for mysticism and for the believing adventure of the individual. But this conversion is not easy. The other articles show just how difficult it is.

Under the title 'Spirituality in the New Age of Recolonization', Sebastian Kappen develops the idea that the cultural, dogmatic and legal construction of the Christian religion in the West has produced a non-God. In his view, the tasks of the liberation theologians were to deconstruct this non-God by a return to the original encounter with Jesus and the divine. However, he thinks that this return to the sources of Christianity is not enough. What we need is an encounter with the ultimate source, since only this source is unconditional and without mediation; it alone makes possible an encounter with the divine here and now. It is this presence always and already given which opens human desire to the spiritual life.

Willigis Jäger, in his article entitled 'Flight from the World or Responsibility for the World?', investigates the narrowness of the self when it is separated from the awareness of belonging to the world. The author argues for a cosmic consciousness open to the trans-personal, since today it is through the desire to go beyond the frontiers of the self that a way is indicated towards a cosmic and mystical religion. This is at the heart of every religion, but the rational reinterpretations have hidden this dimension. Its present reappearance impels us to think of our tradition in this new space without an inflation of the individual and without fusion in the All. From this framework the author traces with originality and passion what he conceives of as a way leading to mysticism.

Jean-Claude Sagne devotes his article to the renewal of the church by the mystical way. He bears witnesses to the extreme importance of scripture among the great spiritual figures, and shows with much depth that the role of the church is one of companionship in welcoming the Word, so that this bears fruit among all in the knowledge and love of Christ. In the gift of scripture transformed into word by the ever present action of the Spirit the institution possesses the energies which allow it to discern and to accompany. On one condition: that it takes more interest in the access of believers to the experience of God than in itself.

With Victor Codina we enter the sphere of information. With much honesty the author spells out the human and spiritual difficulties of the base communities in Latin America. The new political and ecclesial context, the challenges from the charismatic groups and from the new religious movements, have caused a crisis. Religious enthusiasm combined with militant life has led to some disillusionment. It is also necessary to invent a wisdom for the time in which the excessive hopes of yesterday, both for the church and the world, have died down. This unforeseen situation is leading to the introduction of a prophetic force which is both politically more realistic and more radical in a Christian way. It has to construct an alternative to a society and a church which run the risk of being content with mediocrity.

Gustavo Gutiérrez establishes the legitimacy of this alternative way by demonstrating that there is a complicity in the gospel between the marginalized and the disciple. God is bound to the outcast. So it is from this divine God that one has to find the foundation for a spirituality which is not that of either exile or flight, but prophetic in its practical options.

With Sebastian Painadath we come to a fine effort by Indian Christians to integrate the traditions of the ashrams into their quest for God. After giving a precise description of this heritage he shows what original spiritual riches can be gained if it is introduced against a Christian horizon. Christianity does not impose external rules, but takes up the internal movement of this practice. Painadath does not conceal the difficulties of this quest, which is necessarily incomplete. It is important for him above all to show the new way which opens up here.

It remains for Gérard Rolland to bring out to some degree the sense of distance between the mystical way and the institution. With much finesse he is guided by an understanding of the need for the institution in Christianity and its radical limit. Mystical witness, silent among the majority, does not cease to say to the institutional body: 'you are not everything'. It is in the interval separating mysticism from the institutional body that the desire of God is kindled.

This winding course, without a pre-established unity, will seem difficult to some readers. If they have the patience to keep on reading, the institution will appear in a new light, because it is situated in the truth that it is not the 'kingdom'.

Christian Duquoc
Gustavo Gutiérrez

The Christian Rule of Mystical Experience

Yves Cattin

The title of this article is doubly provocative, since one can hardly talk of a rule in connection with an experience which presents itself primarily as one that escapes all rules. And a mystical experience – perhaps like all subjective experiences – cannot subject itself to a rule. As experience, it recognizes only the rule of freedom which institutes it and inspires it, even if in other respects, from the outside, it is judged, approved or condemned in the name of the values which claim to impose themselves on it. On the other hand, to the degree that this experience presents itself as being mystical, it has God as its object. Or perhaps it would be better to say that God is its subject and that God takes the believer as object. In this respect this experience evades all measurement, since its object is that which has no common measure.

However, the problem of the rule of mystical experience appears when mystics begin to speak and undertake to communicate their experience. In so doing they involve their experience in a first externality by agreeing to submit it to the rules of language, to the rules of the grammar and syntax of our common languages, and more generally to the rules of communication. Even if mystics try to urge their tongues to say what they do not usually say, in the end of the day they are agreeing to subject their experience to the rules of the linguistic community. If they do not agree, mystics condemn themselves to silence. In this silence their experience ceases to be problematic; it evades all judgment and no criticism can touch it. If, on the contrary, mystics begin to talk, then they agree in advance to subject their experience to the rules of common language.

If in being communicated this experience is confessed as a Christian experience, it must then allow itself to face a second externality, more formidable than that of language. In announcing and stating that it is an experience of God, mystical experience claims a truth which is that of God's own self. And often in involuntarily forgetfulness of the historical and psychological conditions which give it birth, this experience in a way presents itself as a new word of God. Then, without always being clearly aware of the fact, mystical experience finds itself under the obligation to be measured by the word of God of which the Christian community has been instituted the guardian from the beginning. For this community, the God who reveals himself in the word of scripture does not say just anything, nor can one make him say just anything. Every mystical experience which claims to be Christian is also required to be submitted to the demands of the orthodoxy and orthopraxy of the Christian community.

So there is a paradox in mystical experience. As experience, it proves both ineffable and incontestable. It knows that it is put in question, but it is then vowed to silence. If this experience undertakes to speak of the God who visits it, then it appeals, at the very heart of the most profound subjectivity, to a truth and an objectivity which are those of God's own self. It appears in the space of language and has to agree to face a twofold otherness, that of the rules of the language which puts it into words (rules which are both grammatical and ethical), and that of the word of God and the way in which it is brought to bear in the community of believers.

So it seems necessary to describe this paradox of mystical Christian experience and to try to formulate the rules to which this experience subjects itself in advance, rules which allow it to confess itself as a Christian experience. This is not just a technical study, since what is at stake in the debate seems to be of the utmost importance. Beyond the truth of the mystical experience itself is the issue of the coherence and cohesion of the Christian community. The question is above all that of the future of the word of God in human history.

I. The paradox of mystical experience

The journey

When mystical experience puts itself into words, it proclaims itself first of all as an experience outside the places known and recognized by our common Christian experiences. When these are expressed in terms of the incarnation of Christ, mystical experience lays claim to an elsewhere, a no-place, or a place in which it is impossible for human beings to stand.

So the mystical experience presents itself as a journey of initiation in the strict sense of the word, a journey of beginning and beginnings. By deliberately leaving all common places, the mystic goes towards an elsewhere which is beyond all known places, a place outside, always experienced and described as a no-place.

The mystical story which tells of this journey uses both spatial words, about the way, and temporal words, about the expectation. And in it we find again the major stages of human existence. There is a foundation event, which is like birth, and in this event everything is already given and everything remains to be done. This event takes place in discontinuity: something happens and one does not know what it is; but it is never what one expects. In this amazement and this surprise believers are torn away from their spiritual well-being or their proud sufficiency, and then they go forward from one break to another. Rather than entering into a new life or a new knowledge, believers set out recognizing what has suddenly and definitively been given to them in the foundation event. Mystics do not end up by recognizing 'afterwards' the God who has come to visit them. They find themselves in the posture of Elijah whom God visits on Horeb; because no one can see God face to face without dying, when Yahweh passes in the gentle breeze Elijah sees only 'his back', when Yahweh has already passed. So the mystic sets out on an impossible pilgrimage, a lost quest. And that would be a vain quest, condemning believers to despair, had they not already received at the beginning of their experience what they undertook to seek and to realize. The prayer of mystics is always that of St Augustine: 'Give me the strength to seek you, since you have made me find you.'[1] St Bernard explains this perfectly in his *Treatise on the Love of God*: 'No one would know how to seek you unless he had first found you; so that you want us to find you in order to seek you and to seek you in order to find you.'[2]

However, this circularity of the mystical experience is only an apparent one. Subject to time like any other experience, mystical experience invents a history which presents itself as a history of the soul with God and a history of God with the soul. But this history constantly runs the risk of compromising God. The mystical experience is also constantly forced into an unsurmountable contradiction. Claiming to be an experience of God, it proves always to be an inadequate experience of God; it denies itself as a true experience of God, constantly emphasizing its impotence in experiencing God.

This contradiction can be surmounted only in an affirmation of the transcendence of God beyond any imaginable transcendence. The God who is experienced is not the greater nor even the Very Great; he is always 'greater' than one can think or imagine, than anything that one can experience. God is always beyond what can be attained in the highest experience. So mystical experience only takes on its contradictory character by escaping 'upwards', losing itself in the affirmation of the transcendence of God who is always 'greater'. As experience of God, it is always surpassed by God, it is always lacking God.

So we will not be surprised to see this experience expressed in the words of desire. The basic and explicatory category of mystical experience is in fact that of a lack. Believers always lack the God whom they always attain only in a presence which lacks something. In their experience, God is always lacking and therefore there is a lack everywhere. The words of desire press in; they accumulate to express the emptiness of the lack of the fullness of God which is experienced in mystical experience. In one of the finest texts of mystical desire, the first chapter of the *Proslogion*, Anselm of Canterbury uses the crudest words of biological need to express this lack which keep desire on edge. Adam in friendship with God 'burped with satiety' in eating 'the bread of angels', while we 'sigh with hunger', we 'go begging' and 'wretchedly desire'.[3] So the believer enters into the infinite dialectic of an infinite desire. This lack is what makes the mystic never know when to stop. Mystical experience is not defined in terms of ecstasy, but rather in terms of exile or exodus. The mystical desire, always unquiet and restless, in that kind of 'violent quietude' of which Pseudo-Dionysius speaks, thus invents a story of stories, and begins to speak.

The mystical word

It is this groaning of infinite desire which gives birth to the mystical word. And at the heart of the most profound and incommunicable subjectivity there appears the concern to communicate this experience to others in the objectivity of language.

First of all, this word seems as it were to break in. Despite themselves, believers begin to speak of their experience. It is rather as if the mute word of desire, prohibited and stupified, became inadequate and appealed to words to express the fullness of God that had been experienced. The mystics speak often, and sometimes they seem to speak too much. But they experience what seems to us to be a lack of discretion as an urgency and a necessity. They know that the splendour of God is not to be spoken and must first be honoured by silence. But they also know that this splendour invests them with an impossible word, a word which is only the sacrament of silence. The mystical word thus undertakes to express what words cannot reveal, what they always hide and veil, the lack of the presence of God. The mystical word, too, does not undertake to expose God but invites us to expose ourselves to God. This is an impossible task for a human word which cannot replace experience but always presupposes it. The mystical word, too, becomes praise and celebration, an invitation to the silence of the loving encounter with God.

Because this word is difficult and precious for the believer, and is compromising for God himself, it calls for the utmost rigour. The mystical word can only be approximate or haphazard, and even if it presents itself as just the beginning, it refuses to say just anything. Nor is it ever, as is often believed, an intoxicated or delirious word; it claims to be a true word which is spoken truth.

This truth of the mystical word which is manifest even in its hesitations is based on the experience that it claims, on the most incommunicable subjectivity. This is one of the paradoxes of mystical experience. One can shrug one's shoulders and reject the validity of this experience. But it does present itself as an experience of God. It thus seems inspired by the most improbable pretension: it presents its very subjectivity as the space of a revelation of the hidden God, this God who reveals himself as the truth itself. Nor is it enough to relate mystical experience to itself by saying that it authorizes itself and thus escapes all judgment. For it is the mystical word itself which appeals to the judgment of God; it enunciates itself, presenting the signs which make it an experience of God.

In fact the mystical word, which appears the most subjective of all words, claims to be a 'new' word of God, a word of the Spirit. As de Certeau remarks, the mystical word is born of a threefold obscurity experienced by the believer. The creation as deciphered by the sciences no longer appears an evident word of God. The text of scripture, delivered over to exegesis, manifests obscurities which make it difficult and often dangerous to read. Finally, ecclesial tradition, which can now be read in an ideological perspective which shows it to be a conflict of real and contradictory powers, is no longer the privileged space in which this word of God is to be heard. One can say that the word of God is exiled from the human world. Mystical believers, too, undertake to go through this threefold obscurity, being open to the heart of adoring subjectivity, to the space for a new word which would be the present word of the Spirit. In the silence of customary voices, the Spirit begins to speak by authorizing an unprecedented word, which from now on is invested with the proclamation of the word of God.

II. The question of the truth of mystical experience

The impossibility or uselessness of talking about mysticism

This unprecedented word of mystical experience, a word which develops in a kind of challenge to the common word, can be understood and comprehended in a critical way. If mystical believers live by the evidence of the truth of the word they have the responsibility to proclaim, the same is certainly not true of those who hear this proclamation. The latter are not engaged in the same journey, and before setting out they ask to be able to study the itinerary of the planned journey. Certainly for their own reasons they can be seduced by the mystical discourse which maintains secret complicities in each of us. But these hearers can also 'ask to see' before going to see.

Now this critical examination always seems disqualified in advance by mysticism itself. The critical discourse which by definition renounces being mystical in order to be solely critical develops by presenting itself as accredited by something other than mystical experience. It can be theological or philosophical reason, psychological analysis, or again the institutional discourse of the authorities in charge of the community. So in advance this discourse would seem doomed to ignorance of the object of which it speaks; it is a discourse which comes from outside, the alien discourse of an alien. Moreover, supposing that this discourse is not only possible but valid, its essential problem is that of its credentials. If this discourse is to be recognized as valid discourse, it needs to be developed on the basis of a critical authority which is accepted both by the one engaged in this discourse and by mystics themselves. In Christianity, this critical authority can only be Christ proclaimed in his gospel as the total and definitive revelation of God. Even if the development of such a criterion presents many difficulties and obscurities, one has to accept that the question of the Christian truth of mystical experience must be posed in the following way: is the God of whom mysticism speaks in its experience the God revealed as Father in Jesus Christ?

To this already considerable difficulty for critical discourse must be added another of a psychological kind. Mystical discourse undertakes to describe an experience. So it is not speculative discourse enunciating theses or truths organized in a corpus or system, even if it is often presented as such. It is above all a narrative discourse which relates a history, and it is nearer to literary or poetical discourse than to philosophical or theological discourse. This discourse is in fact the account of a journey or a traveller relating to us his or her 'homesickness' by describing a country which is ours and yet which we do not know. This account given in a language which is alien to us always needs to be translated for those of us who are not (yet) mystics. We know the considerable effort at translation made by mystical authors like Meister Eckart or St John of the Cross. But in this domain more than elsewhere, every translation is to some degree a betrayal and the critical examination always risks stumbling over translation problems without reaching the reality experienced in mystical experience itself, as is shown by the clashes between Meister Eckart and the theological authorities of his time. And this critical examination is made even more difficult by the fact that each of us continues to have some secret complicity with mystical discourse to which we are to some degree committed, as it were compromised by it. We are not (yet) mystics, but in a way mystical discourse speaks of us, tells about us and puts us in question, explains and disturbs us. And everyone knows the difficulty it has in questioning itself.

The critical demand

All the difficulties referred to here merely emphasize the difficult and somewhat sorry urgency of the critical demand made on Christian mystical experience. I speak of difficulty and pain here because I think that the question of mystical experience and its discernment, and that of the often flaunted claim to this experience, appear only in periods of crisis. I would almost say that there is no such thing as happy mysticism and mystical theology. When Christian experience blossoms in the happiness of being – if that is possible – it does not feel the need to call itself mystical and has no need of critical examination to demonstrate that it is what it announces and confesses. Behind and beyond all discourse, it is what it is, the gospel of a person before God, in the gospel. It is enough to examine the life of the majority of the great believers to convince oneself of this.

If there is a question about mystical experience, it is because first of all there is not one or more mystical experiences, but a mystical claim. What I call 'mystical claim' does not relate primarily to what today is sometimes called the religious renewal and to the taste, which is sometimes a fashion, for mysticisms of every kind, above all from the East. When one looks at Christian history, this desire for new spiritual experiences does not appear either new or significant, however much the Christian tradition seems to be inspired by such experiences. What by contrast is full of meaning is the fact that today these experiences in a general way announce and claim their truth outside and against religious institutions, of whatever kind. This fact, in Christianity at least, needs to be interpreted as an identity crisis experienced by believers in their churches. Since the institutional context has changed radically, believers no longer know who they are; they no longer recognize themselves, in the churches even less than elsewhere. The places of the word of God have become archaic, and Christians have become as it were orphans of this world. It would take too long here to analyse how this loss of identity has come about. The sacred texts have become more and more difficult to read, to such a degree has exegesis revealed their complexity. The religious institutions have been unmasked by the human sciences as places of power and conflict. And theologies have been analysed as so much ideological discourse. Then believers find themselves engaged, not in a renewal, but in an attempt at reconnaisance which leads them to try anything if only they can finally be themselves. There is no longer any absolute relationship with the Absolute, and all the relative truths appear good to confess and live, often provisionally, sometimes – and contradictorily – in great tolerance. Instead of reading and hearing the word of God believers then give themselves the task of expressing themselves and stating what they believe. In this way there is born what I call here the mystical claim.

It is important to emphasize the positive element in such a claim. Every believer is called to another position in faith and reflection on faith. It is almost as if in the obligation to renounce the happy possession of the truths of faith every adult believer saw himself or herself entrusted with the task of producing for the people of our day the truths set out in the word which God addresses to us. For the first time, perhaps, the great majority of Christians in their communities are called not only to the experience of faith, but in this experience to the understanding of faith, to the free and critical presentation of the truth of their faith. The certainties of faith are ceasing to be evident; by contrast, it is the truths of the world which have become so. Faith, which until recently was an impregnable bastion, is ceasing to be a place or a state and has become a road, a way of transit for the word of God in its exodus among human beings. If that is so, faith must undertake to invest all areas of human practice and knowledge, all the areas of human existence. In these areas faith opens up new spaces, spaces of gratuitousness. Thus faith introduces a fragility as an injury or a doubt in these human places by announcing that where everything has been said, or where human beings have undertaken to say everything, there is still something to say which has already been said but which has not yet been heard, a word which has come from God.

So if one wants to receive and analyse in a positive way these new more or less wild practices which are arising almost everywhere, in the churches and outside them, it is important to see that they bear a promise of renewal and life – provided, of course, that they are not the pure expression of more or less delirious subjectivities. And it is here that the critical demand, or, to put it more simply, the necessity of theology, arises. In fact these practices, by more or less rejecting the institutions and authorizing themselves, risk proclaiming only themselves. In presenting themselves as the experience of a God whom no one has ever seen, they can easily become the prey of the illusions and mirages of subjectivity. And the God whom they announce can only be an idol of the self. Even when such experiences claim to be

Christian, they must agree to confront the objectivity and the otherness of the Word of God addressed to the community of believers. For in Christianity God does not speak primarily in secret in the human heart. And when God speaks, as St John of the Cross emphasizes in his Mount Carmel, it is not to say anything other than the word addressed to his people. This word has been consigned to the scriptures and realized in Christ. So there cannot be anything other and more in mystical experience than has already been given in Christ. Christian mystical experience, when it undertakes to speak of itself, thus always appeals to a word which authorizes it: the word of God which is revealed in fullness in Christ.

III. The 'authorized' experience

The temptation of immediacy
    When I talk of 'authorized' mystical discourse or mystical experience it is important not to misunderstand the meaning of the word 'authorized'. There is no question of any authority, even a Christian authority, fixing in advance the framework of mystical experience so that it can be called Christian. When I speak here of authority and authorization, I mean that if mystical experience is to manifest itself in all its truth, when it begins to speak and announce the God who reveals himself in it, it also has the task of stating its source, the event which gives birth to it and the space in which it is deployed. In short, the truth in mystical experience is that of manifesting the God of which it is the trace, who authorizes and authenticates it. If this experience authorizes itself by rejecting the otherness of the one of whom it speaks, then it risks speaking of nothing but itself and the subjectivity which conveys it.

    For in Christian experience, what is called mystical experience appears first of all as a temptation, the temptation of the immediacy of God. In it believers become involved in an apparently contradictory process: for lack of their God, they appeal beyond the lack itself to the fullness of a presence freely and overabundantly given. Believers then run the risk of annexing God, of possessing God and manipulating God for their own enjoyment. The lack then proves to have been supplied, in a kind of illusory plenitude. Here experience imprisons itself in a definitive circularity, and all the more indisputably God is imprisoned there. Mystical experience is also what it proclaims, but it proclaims what it is. It becomes imprisonment in self-sufficiency and solitude; it no longer has anything outside itself; it no longer has anything else.

It is beyond doubt in this presence of the other at the depths of mystical experience that we have to seek the rule for mystical Christian experience. What is the other lack unveiled in mystical experience, and is this other revealed in the cross of Christ?

One can see the gravity and the importance of the question of the rule of mystical experience. It is not just a matter of examining a discourse and its coherence, a discourse which mystics themselves disqualify in advance, announcing it as polysemic, metaphorical and inadequate. It is not just a matter of having and describing an experience which in itself remains ineffable and incommunicable. Far less is it a matter of disciplining an errant subjectivity in the framework of a given institution, integrating it in institutional norms. These more or less avowed intentions can be legitimate, but remain superficial. What is at stake in the question is much more serious in Christianity. It is a matter of the most serious risk for the gospel, the risk run by God's own self as God appears committed and compromised in the highest subjective experience. Every mystical experience contains the risk of idolatry, the risk of a God who is lacked and lacking.

The discernment of mystical experience also consists in investigating its other lack. At the heart of the most profound experience believers have to be reminded of a principle of reality, a principle which is the foundation of the objectivity of Christian experience, of both the individual and the community, and which forbids it both the mirages of the inner life and the illusions of a realization of the kingdom of God in history.

The otherness of the face of God

So mystical experience can claim to be Christian only if it subjects itself to the verification of the basic critical norm of Christian faith. That is possible only if, in advance, it renounces the desire for the immediacy with God of which it dreams and assumes the category of mediation. In speaking of mediation, I mean that the way of eminence or participation, preferred by mystical experience, which often relates it to the henology of Plotinus, must be permanently corrected and as it were rectified by the affirmation at the heart of experience of an irreducible otherness of which subjectivity cannot take account. This principle of otherness prevents mystical experience from unfolding in the absolute positivity of a fully realized desire. By clearly accepting its real failure to possess the God who is always 'greater', the desire takes on the negativity of all human experience of God and is called to a real conversion which is a true death: the desire becomes a 'desire without desire'. The scriptures remind us ceaselessly that no one can see God without dying, and the mystical desire to 'see God' must always accept the obscurity of the cross of Christ.

If applied to the Christian demand, these remarks risk seeming to abstract, and it is important to make them more specific.

Mystical experience, which expresses itself with words of the utmost wisdom or those of 'learned ignorance', always appears as an implementation of the eschatological desire to see God. And when this experience is confessed as Christian, it is called on to renounce realized eschatology in order to accept history and the obscurity of history. If it does not do so, it ceases to be Christian and announces its own end in an always doubtful millenarianism.

So what does it mean to accept history? For an understanding of the originality of the Christian mystical experience it seems to me that three characteristics must be emphasized.

1. The Christian mystical experience supposes that the believer who 'experiences' God exists previously in the hearing of a word. That is another way of saying that this experience could not claim to by-pass faith and go beyond it. Faith is the sphere in which all Christian experience, including mystical experience, is deployed. And the word heard and received in faith makes believers capable of inventing in turn a word which responds to the word addressed to them and initiates a new practice which realizes this word. If mystical experience is so obstinate about seeing by refusing and ceasing to believe, it ceases to understand the word and hears only itself. That would not be so important if in doing this it did not abandon the world to its violence and its misery. Christian mysticism, when remains in faith, is not then one that sees or has visions, but one that 'hears'. It does not see anything, but it hears, and what it hears transforms all its existence and the world in which it lives.

2. Christian mysticism must be described more specifically, because when believers consent to hear the word of God, they risk having illusions. There is in fact no guarantee that the word heard is that of God and not that of a delirious subjectivity. Also, in Christianity, the word of God always manifests itself as a strange word which dispossesses believers of their lives and puts them under an obligation. This is what we call grace, the basic category of human existence: if it is to become Christian, human existence, which has the reasons and the meaning that it gives itself, is called to become a stranger to itself, outside its *raisons d'être*, to exist in the gratuitousness of a gift. And if it is true that for Christians the word of God is achieved in Jesus Christ, then mystical experience, like all Christian experience, is called to exist from the strange existence of Jesus, 'who did

not count equality with God a thing to be grasped, but emptied himself, taking the form of a servant, being born in the likeness of men'.[4] And the servant Jesus went as far as death on a cross. Mystical experience, too, is called to this 'glory of the cross'. It can only bear witness to the presence of God by stripping itself of itself. Then by ignoring itself and abandoning false human knowledge, it enters into the wisdom of God.

3. If mystical believers are ready to enter into the obscurity of this abasement; if they agree, as Meister Eckart asks, not only to be poor but even to be poor with his poverty, then they effectively renounce the immediacy of God of which their experience gives them the illusion: they are called on to forget the ever-fragile states of an injured subjectivity. They enter into history, and this history requires intermediaries which set up in the world the presence of an absent God. In a way, Christian mysticism is always eucharistic, invested with a sacramentality that calls for the realization of the kingdom which comes about in work for justice.

But the gesture of Christ in his death and resurrection indicates an even more precise way for Christian mystical experience. In fact, in this obligation to history and justice the mystical desire no longer encounters a God who calls himself the absolute, the wholly other or the inaccessible. It encounters a God who is always beyond, 'greater', at the very heart of our life. The scriptures of the New Testament indicate that for us God can be identified as Father and his son Jesus, whom he gives and abandons. And in turn Jesus gives himself in the death of the cross, by giving up his life; it is in this abandonment that St John sees the place of the manifestation of the glory of God. So the transcendence of God is a transcendence of abandonment and a transcendence of exchange. The new scriptures, with formidable logic, invite us to recognize God, and to encounter him, in the abandonment, in all those who are abandoned, 'the poor, the widow and the orphan'. It is here that mystical experience, which lays claim to the utmost interiority (God *intimior intimo meo*), is obliged to the greatest externality, the greatest otherness. The God whom it senses in the deepest interiority points it towards encounter with others, obliges it to approach others to make them neighbours. There alone, in the face of the other, can the face of God be recognized. The holy and transcendent God can only be encountered if the other person is welcomed in the proximity of the neighbour. There alone God exposes himself by calling for ethical responsibility. So mystical experience cannot close in on itself. It cannot even present itself as the supreme experience or the supreme perfection of the Christian experience. Like all Christian experience, it is addressed by this discreet and silent word which speaks in the face of the other. Called to this transcendence of abandonment and humility, it can then recognize the face of God which comes to visit it.

Mystical experience and the community of believers

So what definitively 'authorizes' the mystical Christian experience is this transcendence of God recognized in the face of the other. This externality can seem unbearable to mystical experience, which thus appears relativized and related to an otherness which it aims to suppress (without recognizing that this experience is thus called to another conception of the transcendence of God than that of the Absolute and the Wholly Other). But it seems that in Christianity this commitment to ethics in the recognition of the other is the necessary condition for the disqualification of all the idols.

However, mystical experience is called to an even greater humility. It is committed to another exteriority, which emerges as the guarantee of this first exteriority of God, visiting the face of the other. Here I want to talk of this exteriority represented by the community of believers, the church.

When God reveals himself, God calls on a people to become his people, the people of God, in a covenant of friendship. And if God speaks of a person, it is always to suggest to him or her a word in the service of God's people. Christian faith, which takes the way of the scriptures, bears witness to the historical event of the word of God in the people of Israel. And first Israel, then the Christian community, have been made guardians of this way of the scriptures. Certainly, God speaks to whomsoever he wills and when he wills, and his word can take the course of believing subjectivities. These particular revelations are infinitely respectable, but they are and remain particular. If they undertake to call and confess themselves Christian, then they agree to conform to the norm of the scriptures. And this norm is guarded and constantly verified in the tradition of the Christian community, with all the hopes and demands, but also the imperfections and faults which this community bears at a given moment of its history.

So Christian mystical experience maintains a compulsory relationship with the church of believers. One can see in this enforced relationship a desire for control on the part of an institution which perceives individual mystical experience (and not only that) as a danger to the institutional order or the body of truths which it is committed to proclaim. We know that the church, like any other institution, secretes a certain form of intolerance by finding it difficult to accept any form of experience which has not been domesticated and normalized.

These analyses can be precise in a number of situations. They show only that the church is not yet completely the church of Christ, a community of men and women freed from the violence of the world by the Spirit of Christ. It also seems to me that this compulsory reference of all Christian experience, including mystical experience, to the authority of the church has a much deeper significance. For the community of believers it is a matter of confessing that in Jesus of Nazareth is realized the fullness of the revelation of God, a revelation of which the community is the guardian and which it celebrates in the eucharist. That necessarily implies that human beings encountered by God, wherever they may be, whatever their particular situations and experiences, experience what they experience in the space opened up by this revelation of God in Jesus Christ. So the Christian community does not claim the right to judge mystical experience. It is this experience, which claims to be Christian experience, that puts itself in the space of Christian experience and is judged by it. The community simply states the place of this experience, attests its authenticity and authority in relation to a word read and understood in the church's tradition.

That having been said, we can specify the exact role of this ecclesial authority. In all the religious tradition, mystical experience encounters 'authorities' which authenticate it or disqualify it. However, it seems to me that the Christian community plays an original role in connection with mystical experience, precisely because of the particular conception that it has of the revelation of God. The essential function of ecclesial authority as compared to mystical experience seems to me to be that of welcoming this experience by asking that it should not be shut in on itself and by considering it as the absolute of all experience, excluding other experiences of Christian life. The lack of God 'who is the greatest', which is attested so strongly in mystical experience, cannot be made good by a single experience or a single type of experience. On the contrary, this lack calls for the multiplicity and the wealth of all experiences, those of the past, present and future. So authority calls on mystical experience to show brotherhood and sisterhood, hospitality to others. In making itself guardian of the plurality that is needed, authority reveals itself as the guarantor of the only unity possible, that of love, which not only rejects identity but demands and maintains otherness.

The role of authority also proves more important than one might imagine. By reminding mystical experience of brotherhood and hospitality, authority allows this experience to unfold as it is, a unique and ineffable experience of encounter with the God of Jesus Christ. This experience, far from seeming to be authorized by the church, discloses the one who gives authorization, the one who inspires and informs the freedom of which it is the supreme expression. And authority, far from limiting this experience by giving it a framework, is by contrast what makes it possible for it to become real, for the incommunicable to communicate itself. Thus authority opens up a real future for this experience, allowing it to go beyond what has been experienced of the God who is 'always greater'. Then mystical experience ceases to be its own truth and its own verification, disclosing the truth of the authority which is its foundation and its source. And if that does not happen, it is because experience cannot confess itself Christian or the authority which authorizes it is no longer Christian.

So one could say that the essential role of authority is to emphasize, in mystical experience, that which it always lacks, that 'without which' it cannot call itself mystical. This experience is an authentic experience of God if it still and always shows that it lacks God and that nevertheless God is the one without whom this experience could not exist and believers could not live. And the function of authority is to prevent mystical experience from existing in a happy positivity, as if it were the vision of God. Authority also reveals that mystical experience is always a wounded experience, directed towards the one who brought it into being and whom it always lacks. It is the experience of those believers who, at the depths of their lives, know that they cannot live without this God whom they always lack.

Conclusion

If these analyses are right, one might conclude that regardless of its original expressions in the subjectivities of believers, mystical experience is the perfection of Christian experience. It too cannot present itself as the supreme expression of the desire for the absolute, which is always a desire for the self and the idol of the self. It is a conversion of this desire, which is a renunciation of the desire itself. Far from being the apotheosis of the inner life or of interiority, by contrast it is as it were an 'extra-territorialization' of believing existence: human beings cease to exist in the face of themselves and their desires, in the face of the world and the idols of the world, to exist in the face of God. Christians do not enter into communion with God either in a desire to lose themselves in him or in a desire to rediscover and realize themselves in him. It is in the forgetfulness of self born of divine forgiveness, in the silence of Abraham on the way to Mount Moriah to sacrifice Isaac, in the dance of Francis of Assisi inventing all the songs of the world, that believers encounter their God, abandoning subjectivity to its own, multiple and contradictory movement. Believers are maintained in faith, and it is there that God comes to encounter them. And God does not encounter them because they have high thoughts or 'spiritual states', but because they refuse to enter into the order of the world, living out an active solidarity with those who, as beggars or stateless persons, have nowhere to lay their head. God is in this alliance with humiliated human beings, which turns things completely upside down. So the transcendence of God is not given in an absolute of life or thought, but is welcomed in the gesture which makes me exist for the other. All the rest is still and indeed always insufficient for transcendence.

Thus God indicates his presence in what it is not, the humiliated humanity of Jesus and the other. And, as Meister Eckart writes, 'even if that is called ignorance, this ignorance leads you and takes you outside all that is known and outside yourself'. Mystical experience is the supreme testimony to this ignorance and this humility in which all Christian existence takes place. At that point there can be born, always provisional and fragile, those moments of happiness which mystical literature loves to describe. Those moments, which aspire to becoming states, are always fortuitous and furtive, like happiness itself; they always appear as though they were 'thrown in', and they are like the poem which crowns language with splendour. But they always relate to the common word which indicates the need to work for justice.

So in mystical experience, believers experience their infinite poverty. God comes to them, and they want to lose themselves in God, and God always points them to others. Mystical experience is always also a sacrifice. In it believers learn to renounce their poverty, accepting themselves for just what they are, in the splendour of the presence of God. In this abasement and this humility, in this silence of being nothing and having nothing to give, believers thus exist only in the amazed welcome of God who is always 'greater'. Mystical experience is only the stripping off of being in the presence of the one who alone gives being.

Then there break into our lives the dawns of the praise and prayer which celebrate the beauty of God and also our impotence to celebrate. Then we love the loved one, whom we also love with that in us which does not love.

Translated by John Bowden

Notes

1. St Augustine, *De Trinitate*, 15, 28, 51.
2. St Bernard, *De diligendo Deo*, 7.22.
3. Anselm of Canterbury, *Proslogion*, ch. 1.
4. Philippians 2.6–7.

Mysticism and the Crisis of Religious Institutions

Carlo Carozzo

The hypothesis underlying these reflections is that the mystical tendencies emerging in advanced industrial societies express a cultural change which the historical religions either have not accepted or cannot accept; thus, their crisis makes it easier to look for the Absolute outside their institutional ambit.

I hope to be able to show the relevance of this hypothesis by going on to draw some of its consequences at a pastoral level.

I. Context and needs

The cultural climate of postmodernity

The end of the totalitarian ideologies of progress – of a Marxist, liberal and even Christian stamp – has been expressed at a cultural level by the disintegration of the two pillars on which the trust of modernity was based, i.e. the certainty of a continuous *progress*, and 'faith' in *science*, regarded as the dimension of rationality capable of resolving the problems which were gradually emerging. Nowadays, it is progress or development and science which have become problematical, and are raising serious questions. So much so that the future which is opening up is one of uncertainty and disquiet.

With this 'end' and 'disintegration' the postmodern era which we are entering is dawning. It is a time of 'disenchantment' with previous ambitions; a time of the feminine paradigm, which is pervading society and attaching more importance to psychological and intuitive dimensions than to rational and material dimensions; a time of fragmentation and an indefinite pluralism after that of solidly unitary cultures; a time of 'weak thought':[1] reason now seems weak, sometimes impotent to direct historical processes and incapable of grasping the foundation of reality and life. The 'strong' values of modernity are being pulverized; others are emerging, but they are fluid, often more vague perceptions and sometimes sensations than well developed convictions with deep roots.

A cultural void is opening up which tends to become filled with a 'pragmatic' philosophy in which solutions are chosen to the degree that they serve to achieve specific ends rather than because of their foundations. There is a mentality of 'enjoyment' of the good things which happen to be on offer at the present; a notion of 'contamination' between ideas of differing provenance, now in the sense of dialogue, now in the sense of syncretism.[2] There is a culture of the 'present': what counts is today, and sometimes, especially in youth culture, the moment.

With the end of what Lyotard calls the 'great stories', the individual retreats into the private sphere, even more immersed in solitude, anonymity and the emotional desert of technological society, often terrified of a future which presents a threatening face. The sense of dissatisfaction is becoming more widespread and is even becoming malaise, a discomfort with life. In the age of weak thought, individuals also discover that they are fragile, thirsty for the happiness continually on offer from the media, and therefore in search of 'a good time today', out to discover a practical way out of the sense of bewilderment which they have developed in the great confusion of a world which seems to them to be splintered, dispersed, out of control.[3] No wonder that many of our contemporaries are trying to achieve existential 'well-being' through numerous disciplines and practices, reacting to the talk of catastrophe.

In this mobile, segmented, individualistic, hedonistic climate of 'weak ontology', various existential expedients have been developed to confront the dissatisfaction or the discomfort at life and discover a meaning to existence. Among them is the re-emergence of religion in a complex and varied form. Manifestations range from the return of traditions belonging to religious folklore (festivals, processions, visits to sanctuaries, etc.), to the rediscovery of the sacred, fundamentalism, the rediscovery of mysticism. Religion seems to be one of the ways of becoming reconciled to oneself, to others, to nature and rediscovering the world as a place which can be lived in 'poetically'.

Features of mysticism

1. Perhaps the deepest need is that of freedom in the quest for the Absolute. Each person wants to follow his or her own path, go his or her own way, without accepting prearranged routes.

2. Mysticism is a quest which is an *experience*, in which the individual is

directly involved, as happens for example in Yoga or meditation, and not the passive recipient of a doctrine. So it is an event which brings with it a taste of life.

3. Precisely because of the importance of experience, what is equally important is *feeling*, emotion, vibrant, intense perception, the peaceful sense of being immersed in a current of life which restores the body, the senses, as organs for the encounter with the Absolute.

4. This does not mean the exclusion of the intelligence, a fall into a total irrationalism, even if this also happens. However, the human organ for grasping the 'divine' is not the reason, nor even theological rationality, but *intuition*, regarded as the only faculty which makes it possible to grasp the divine directly, through contact.

5. The aim of mysticism is the overcoming of the limits of the human condition, in particular and pragmatically those of everyday city life which is repetitive and draining, by achieving *union with the cosmos* perceived as a whole, a living organism and not a cold mechanism in the style of Newton, and *with the depths of the self*, the 'supreme self' where the divine is present, if it is not itself part of the divine. These two features – a sense of the world as a whole and the journey towards the depths of one's own subjectivity[4] – indicate the trend and the experimentation towards a free experience of cosmic and mystical unity which it is achieved through the intuition of the divine at the root of the 'self' which offers serenity, peace, reconciliation and well-being, bringing freedom from fear, or from reality, from the discomfort of living in solitude and in alienation. It would seem more correct to speak here of panentheism[5] than of pantheism: the world is in God and God is in the world in a kind of 'perichoresis'.

II. Mysticism and the institution

Relations with the institution as such . . .

As we know from history, relations between mysticism and the institution, between charisms and the institution, have never been easy. For the most part the mystics have been viewed with mistrust, have been considered potentially heterodox individuals who cannot be controlled, disturbers of the institutional order. The difficulties Christians who were later considered saints had with the institutional church is well known. But afterwards . . . !

On the other hand, the mystical experience brings with it a stimulus towards by-passing the institution, which tends to set itself up as an intermediary in relations with the Absolute. At the least, the institution tends to control scrupulously the truthfulness and credibility of mystical experience and its compatibility with official 'doctrine', whereas the mystic moves towards a direct, immediate encounter with the deity.

There is truth in what Gerhardus van der Leeuw writes in his classic of the phenomenology of religion: 'For mysticism, every detail, all the particulars, all the historical elements of religion are in the end a matter of indifference . . . Mysticism speaks the language of all the religions, but no religion is essential to it . . . The incarnation of God which is the very heartbeat of Christianity can finally become for the mystic no more than a parable which reflects his or her own lot, an eternal generation in the heart of human beings.'[6]

. . . and with the institution in crisis today

The tension that already exists as a tendency becomes rejection and above all alienation when an institution in crisis is confronted with *this* mysticism now coming to birth, which is no longer just the experience of some individual, which has always existed, but today has spread with a notable density and thus has acquired social relevance.

In the present situation the perception of their own crisis which has come about in the religious institutions has produced alarm and fear which set in motion *mechanisms of self-defence* to protect them from the risk of being marginalized in the flow of history and thus becoming irrelevant. These mechanisms are in essence two: on the one hand *rigidity directed inwards*, and on the other *suspicion directed outwards*: the world appears as a hostile and decadent place and thus provokes either on the one hand reactions typical of the victim who complains of the obstacles, real or supposed, presented by society, or the indifference of society, or on the other an accentuation of the fear that ideas coming from the world will infiltrate into church communities, polluting doctrine and provoking deviant behaviour.

As a result, self-defence aggravates the tendency to resort to the principle of authority in an attempt to exercise stricter control over the members of the institution, increasing the warnings and the denunciation of the dangers, and the rise of heterodox ideas and the behaviour which accompanies them, in contradiction to doctrine. Because of this defensive stance and the rigidity which goes with it, the institution for the most part becomes incapable of being attuned to postmodern cultural sensitivities so as to be able to identify relevant questions, filter them and attempt to offer a response. The result is 'strong' ideals and 'weak' subjects, definitive formulations addressed to unsettled people with many problems, and therefore a real paradox of incommunicability. And there is a further paradoxical concentration on morality expressed for the most part in didactic terms, whereas God remains in the background, precisely when the spiritual question, embryonic and vague and even confused though it may be, is presented as the pre-eminent interest.

Furthermore, an institution in crisis tends to affirm vigorously a 'strong' identity, so that when confronted with this mysticism it either opposes it directly or attempts to take it over: it gives space to mysticism, but by annexing it, colonizing it, with the argument that its own mystical tradition is purer and superior. This only increases the mistrust of those who are in search of the divine.

On the other hand, if the tendencies of the institution are already a problem for the mystic, they become even more problematical in the present context. The evidence for this seems to me to be clear if we compare the essential features of the mysticism which is developing with the present-day reality of the religious institutions, even though this is not the same everywhere.

Anyone who is in search of the Absolute in freedom finds for the most part a vast, complicated, rigid orthodoxy which issues warnings backed by authoritarian threats;
rather than the possibility of a spiritual experience there is a stress on the primacy of the propositions of faith;
rather than 'feeling' and beauty there are normally cold liturgies which leave those attending them passive;
rather than intuition the central feature is theological rationalism.

So, rightly or wrongly, mysticism finds in the religious institution an obstacle to its quest; again, rightly or wrongly, it is aware of the inevitable risk of being corrupted to the point of being made subservient to the institution's need to perpetuate itself and exercise a domination which seeks to bring it into line, to normalize it, to control it for institutional ends of self-perpetuation and, if possible, expansion. However, in all probability at the root of this is yet another motif: the very image of God.

A contrast in the images of God

I believe that the most evident aspect of the God of this mysticism is the quest for a *present God*, a God beyond the concept; a call, rather, to the sense of mystery: a God worshipped within or beyond the framework of reality and the depth of the self of which God is the spirit, in the very intensity of the emotion experienced in God's presence. 'A veiled return to Neoplatonism',[7] experienced in the form of oceanic and cosmic feelings, a rehabilitation of the sacred and the religious 'in a non-inclusive mystical vision',[8] this God is a challenge to the 'Apollonian God, the God of measure, of balance, of reason, and even, in a rather more veiled way, the

God of the rationalistic theology of the last twenty years, to recover a God who is closer to us and more human, more sensitive to our sufferings and more in keeping with our spiritual anxieties'.[9] By contrast, the God of the religious institution appears distant and separate, imprisoned in rigid concepts, and hence is perceived as lifeless.

The quest is for an encounter with a 'maternal' God who brings help, who takes to heart the pain of his creatures, a God who can restore the increasingly sick psyches of our urban world, a God with feminine traits of watchful tenderness who brings healing from the anxiety, indeed the anguish, of life. By contrast, the God of the religious institutions is worshipped as an authoritarian figure, caught up in an astral transcendence; a severe father God who governs events from on high with a justice which sees only black and white and who is not guided by a boundless love; a God who holds us guilty and does not give us breathing space, thus becoming the cause of a further anguish. From this perspective we need to ask whether the rejection of a pastoral approach dominated by fear, whose existence over the centuries has been amply documented by Delumeau, 'too gloomy a pastoral approach, is not one of the causes of the "Dechristianization" of the West'.[10]

In the last resort, in this mystical vision, as moreover is characteristic of this whole religious trend, there is a move to go beyond the tension between subject and object in the perspective of the union between God, human beings and nature, among whom there is an exchange of cosmic energy, offered generously and without asking anything in return: a kind of 'grace without force',[11] freed from the burden of conversion. On the contrary, the God of the Christian churches is regarded as deriving from a continuous dualism, because this God is thought to be based on an opposition between God and the world, body and Spirit, natural and supernatural, subject and object. Thus Christianity is held to be responsible, along with science (which was not fortuitously born in a Christian cultural climate), for having contributed historically towards fragmenting, shattering, parcelling up, increasing human suffering. So at root there seems to be a contrast between images of God: the God of the institutions is not interested; and because an institution in crisis tends to make the vision of God rigid and to emphasize the rigour of the criteria for belonging, making them over-specific in the doctrinal and moral sphere, it paradoxically contributes towards forcing the quest for the Absolute outside its own ambit.

III. Challenge or question?

The fears of the institutions

Certainly, many problems are raised by this emerging sensitivity. They need the clear examination that they are being given in this issue of *Concilium*. It may in fact be that here we have *two valuable mystical experiences which are not identical*, as is emphasized by Sudbrack, referring to a distinction made by Rahner.[12] Be this as it may, simply by recognizing the importance of the rediscovery of the spiritual, the churches have been alarmed by the spread of this mystical tendency, are afraid of its infectiousness and see it as a danger. So they point to its syncretistic character, the religious relativism in which any religion is acceptable provided that it makes people 'feel better', the loss of a sense of truth in the name of a freedom which is both vague and arbitrary, the frustration of the decisive importance of conversion. Thus Cardinal Poupard regards this as a 'return of paganism', as he said in a lecture given in Genoa on 27 November 1992.[13]

So is this mysticism to be understood as a challenge? Is it a rival to the churches, with which it is in competition? Is it vital to preserve Christian people from the danger of infection through greater doctrinal and ethical preparation?

'Challenge' or 'blessing'?

In my view another interpretation of this religious sensitivity, of which the New Age is the most significant expression, is more relevant and more fertile at a pastoral level. It is one proposed by Terrin, who in fact refuses to see it as a challenge because *it simply represents the fruit of postmodern culture in its religious reflections*.[14] It should be noted that it has not in fact arisen from a conflict between the religions. It is not opposed to any of the organized religions. Rather, it expresses the spirit of an age in which there is a 'radical difference between the mode of practice of traditional religion and the changed cultural context'.[15]

Thinking in terms of challenge in fact leads to a defensive attitude, one of 'closing the ranks', which makes others enemies to be guarded against, instead of first being prepared to listen to others in order to decipher the possible significance of their presence and the questions which they can bring.

Certainly there is a challenge, but, in being challenged, it seems to me that the religious institutions are merely being provoked to ask what new features, if any, are expressed in the new religious sensibility, whether the message it is addressing to our faith is a new one, and if so how. These questions need to be asked so that we can at least begin to understand those postmodern people who appear, admittedly not in great numbers, in our ranks. Might this not be a 'sign' through which the Spirit of Jesus is addressing itself to the churches?

The meaning for us? Rediscovering the mystical status of faith

It is always very difficult to interpret an event, and arbitrariness in interpretation is easier to fall into than one might think. That being said, at all events it seems to me that if the analysis made above is reasonably correct, postmodern mysticism is an invitation to change pedagogical key and in particular *to put experience of the God of Jesus rather than propositions at the centre of religious education*. This should be done, not to respond to an attack, nor as a precaution, but in order to be positively faithful to the heart of the Christian faith, where God communicates himself to us in the power of the Spirit, as we know from Christian beginnings.

Unless Christians today, and even more tomorrow, in the pluricultural world which is taking shape, are in a position to say 'I believe' on the basis of personal experience, an experience of God however limited, and therefore almost incapable of being thematized, I do not see how they can cope with the clash with society in which we are increasingly involved. A faith without profound roots in the self, a faith which is not personalized, will find it very difficult to avoid the risk of being reduced to a set of beliefs, a religious knowledge which may be well organized but is not sustained or fed by a spiritual experience. And in that case, will not it be built on sand?

A faith which rediscovers its mystical status is clearly not an alternative to the doctrinal dimension, and it would be fatal if it fell into a rash subjectivism. But it is only within and thanks – by grace – to a spiritual experience that the codified truths will light up from within, acquiring a savour, becoming significant, vital and fertile. Otherwise we will be tied to the 'letter which kills', to use St Paul's term.

Guidance and dialogue

Consequently, after the use of a method of explanation which is hopefully relevant and lively, it is important to introduce personal guidance.[16] Such guidance will be aware that every story of faith is unique. Every life is unique. The freedom and personalization of our journeys are not a luxury but decisive conditions for the growth of Christian adults in the faith. Certainly teachers are needed, but not teachers who lay down the law, hastily and timidly. The teachers needed are experienced and wise guides, attentive to each person's story and then ready to move aside when individual Christians find themselves facing their God. Like that of every good teacher, their art is one of gradually making themselves superfluous, since no one can interfere in the unique and unrepeatable dialogue between human beings and the God of Jesus, the sole teacher.

Clearly this does not mean abandoning the others to themselves and not helping them to decipher their inner experience of the discovery of the presence of God. Far less does it lead to a 'do it yourself' faith. Dialogue with other Christians is indispensable because we are the church. So too is inter-religious dialogue: the mystics of the different religions have much to say, since they swim in the same deep waters, simply interpreting the divine mystery in different ways.

Be this as it may, it is one thing to learn a religious knowledge according to interpretations which claim to be unique and definitive. It is very different to hold a dialogue between those in search of God who loyally – and playfully – listen to one another, first of all on the basis of their spiritual experience. Doing this one becomes modest and sober in talking of God, and when it is realized that words about God go beyond any experience of God we may have, the inclination is to resort to silence in order to hear and patiently listen to the one whose name transcends all our words, and even our gentlest and most poetic symbols.

Translated by John Bowden

Notes

1. G. Vattimo is the Italian philosopher who has devised the philosophy which he himself has defined as 'weak thought': cf. above all id., *Il pensiero debole*, Milan 1983.

2. For this cf. A Rizzi, *L'Europe e l'altro*, Milan 1992, especially ch.II; id., 'Tra nostalgia e crisi: il terzo uomo', in *Rassegna di teologia*, Rome 1982.

3. In the work mentioned, Rizzi identifies three movements in process of surmounting the crisis: 'a return to the roots, nomadism and the exodus' (45), which he then examines in detail.

4. For more information cf. J. Sudbrack, *La nuova religiosità una sfida per i cristiani*, Brescia 1988, above all ch. 5.

5. The term originated in the discussion of German idealism in the early nineteenth century, and was particularly advocated in process theology, notably by Charles Hartshorne.

6. G. van der Leeuw, *La religion dans son essence et ses manifestations*, Paris 1955, 494.

7. Cf. A. N. Terrin, *New Age, la religiosità del post-moderno*, Bologna 1992, 87.

8. Ibid., 82

9. Ibid., 84.

10. Cf. J. Delumeau, *Le péché et la peur*, Paris 1983, 627.

11. Cf. Terrin, *New Age* (n. 7), 86.

12. In the volume referred to, Rahner writes that the expression of depth in itself as one and infinitely extended and of union with the world are very valuable in human terms, but do not coincide with a mystical experience of God (cf. 301–2).

13. The title of his lecture was: 'Le nuove forme di religiosità e il ritorno del paganesimo: una sfida per la Chiesa'.

14. Cf. Terrin, *New Age* (n. 7), above all ch. VIII.

15. Ibid., 247: his italics.

16. Cf. Adrien Demoustier, 'Experience de Dieu', *Etudes* 10, 1993.

Spirituality in the New Age of Recolonization

Sebastian Kappen

Seen from the Asian point of view,[1] 'the collapse of all utopias' is a convenient myth floated in the West to serve its neo-colonial interests. The seeming justification for this myth is the collapse of the Soviet Union. But that event meant the invalidation of the Soviet version of socialism, not of the socialist utopia as such, whose origin is to be traced back to the Judaeo-Christian hope in the coming of 'the new heaven and the new earth'. Shorn of its obsolete elements, the socialist utopia as envisaged by Marx[2] pointed to a new age in which humans will no more be estranged from nature; in which the product of labour will be the bond of love; in which people will exercise control over the production of goods, the establishment of order, and the creation of ideas and symbols; in which the greatest need of a human being will be the need for his or her fellow humans; in which freedom will be realized less in the production of the useful than in the creation of the beautiful. In short, it will be an age in which humans, bonded by concern for common good and commitment to the creation of beauty, will collectively shape their own future. By its very nature, this is a utopia that cannot perish and will not perish; it can only degenerate or be marginalized or lapse into temporary forgetfulness. And it degenerated not with the collapse of the Soviet Union but with its emergence as a totalitarian regime. Something analogous happened in the history of early Christianity. Christianity's birth as a monarchical institution coincided with the marginalization, if not death, of the prophetic utopia of Jesus. If prophecy survived at all, it was in the interstices of the church or in heretical circles. In fact it was the socialist tradition, especially the one formulated by Karl Marx, that took over the Judaeo-Christian utopia and preserved it for the future. Unfortunately, it too got distorted in the course of time and was jettisoned by Stalinism. This perhaps is the greatest tragedy of the twentieth century. What is more disturbing is the rise of the counter-utopia which Roger Garaudy has called 'the monotheism of the market'. I would rechristen it the monotheism of capital. Capital is the central deity of the new promised land flowing with milk and honey. What is promised is not beatific vision but beatific consumption. The acquisition of ever newer, ever more time-saving, ever more fashionable goods and services is held up as the be-all and end-all of life. It is a consumption that perpetually consumes itself to make room for the more seductive goods yet to come. And where do you find the inexhaustible supply of ever fresh goods and services? Of course, in the market. Implicit here is a new soteriology. The old adage, 'No salvation outside the church', has given way to 'No salvation outside the market'. To propagate this message, the centres of capitalism are sending out missionaries by the thousand to the less industrialized countries of Asia and Africa, not yet fully integrated into the 'saving' sphere of the market. The whole venture has been aptly called recolonization.

The neo-colonialists believe that their success is guaranteed because they have an ultimate secular sanction in the nuclear weapons they have accumulated. For the so-called developing nations the only option is between consumerist utopia or nuclear devastation.

A still greater guarantor of recolonization is the Christian Ungod. I am using the term Christian Ungod to distinguish him from the Divine whom Jesus met. It is the god whom Christians fashioned to legitimize their lust for wealth and power. It is this Ungod who inspired kings and popes to embark on the Crusades and massacre millions of Jews and Turks, who in the person of the Grand Inquisitor indulged in the brutalities of witch-hunting and the burning of heretics, who authorized the Christian kings of the West to colonize and enslave all 'pagan' nations, who gave the green signal to slave trade involving the transportation across the Atlantic of twenty million Africans, who connived at the brutal extermination of the indigenous tribes of the Americas and Australias,[3] who steadied the hands of those who dropped atom bombs over Hiroshima and Nagasaki, who in his new incarnation as an illustrious preacher stood by the side of President Bush in 1991 as the latter knelt down to invoke divine blessing on his projected war on Iraq that was to kill thousands of Iraqis, men, women and children.[4] He is a god who will not hesitate to avenge the death of one North American marine with the death of ten times the number of Somalis. In short, he is a god who takes the side of the affluent against the poor, of the powerful against the weak, a god with hands dripping with the blood of the innocent.

The Ungod is a god of ambivalence. He will exhort humans to love one another, while turning a blind eye to ethnic cleansing, genocide and cluster-bombing. A jealous guardian of the genital morality of the faithful, he is unconcerned about the immorality of exploitation and injustice. He is all zeal for the fate of the unborn, but the born who are doomed to death by systemic violence fail to move his bowels of mercy. He has invested heavily in promoting the fear of sin in the faithful and works up the same fear to such a pitch of intensity that it kills the human in humans more than sin itself.

The construction of the Ungod

The Ungod is the end-result of a long process of the interpretative distortion of an original encounter with the Divine. Its beginning can be discerned already in the creation story of Genesis. There creation is represented as a war between a patriarchal Yahweh and the Waters, the latter being but another name for the great Mother Goddess of neolithic civilization.[5] Later, Israelites would transfer to the same Yahweh their own hatred and vindictiveness against non-Israelite tribes. The same process of reconstructing the Divine can be seen in the New Testament.[6] The Divine Jesus met repudiated all power and castigated all rulers of the world who lord it over their subjects and make them feel the weight of their authority. But with Paul the same god would advise the faithful to obey all authorities since all authority is from him. A crucial stage in reinterpretation was the official teaching that revelation came to an end with the death of the last Apostle and with the closing of the canon in the fourth century. This meant in effect that in and through Christ the Divine uttered the last word and rendered itself superfluous, leaving it to its vicegerents to interpret the 'deposited' Word for generations to come. With that, the Divine was muted once and for all. And the muted Divine is the Divine dead and become Ungod. With the Divine silenced, the church became vociferous and that too with a vengeance, cocksure of the profoundest mysteries of being and non-being, of salvation and damnation, of the destiny of the peoples and nations. No sooner did the Divine congeal into a speechless thing than a brood of theologians sprang up who pounced on it and dissected it into 'clear and distinct ideas', manageable and manipulable. The original command of Yahweh to subdue the earth they interpreted to mean subduing the Divine itself. The Divine was thus reduced to a product, to a commodity that in due course became, like money, the universal equivalent of all commodities.

Jesus, too, was subjected to a similar process of reconstruction.[7] The young prophet from Nazareth who had the audacity to challenge the powers that were and for that reason was done to death was soon metamorphosed into a high priest, and the Jesus-movement into cult-centred religion. With Christianity allying itself with imperial and, later, colonial powers, the same Jesus began to be worshipped as Christ the King, who in that capacity would preside over the conversion of 'pagans'. When, subsequently, the hope of converting the world proved illusory, the same Christ was recycled into the Cosmic Christ, a concept that helped the church theologically to annexe to its own fold all men and women of good will irrespective of race and religion.

The Ungod as the guarantor and legitimizer of the consumerist utopia today holds sway over vast sections of Christians, clerical and lay. He is at once the product and the producer of a particular brand of cult, law, and, above all, theology. But with the explosion of communication, the media have taken over the major part in recyling the Ungod. Seen from another angle, the media have become the mediator, par excellence, between the Ungod and the common run of humans. Somewhat after the manner of the Hindu deity, Krishna, who by divine magic so multiplied himself as to enable him to mate at the same time with his 18,000 brides, so too, thanks to the media, the Ungod can simultaneously make himself visible to all the inhabitants of the planet. Today he is occupying the centre stage of Christianity, if not of world history itself.[8]

If so, where do we go from here? We cannot ride with the Ungod on the crest of the consumerist wave. For the consumerist utopia is in reality dystopian. It spells doom for us Asians since it can sustain itself only by exploiting our cheap physical and mental labour, by coercing us into unequal and discriminatory trade relationships, by infringing our national sovereignty and, above all, by undermining our cultural identity. Consumerism spells doom also for the industrialized nations, a fact borne out by the innumerable symptoms of cultural decay in Western society – the increase in teenage and adult violence, the appalling spread of drug abuse, the break-up of the family, the loss of community, the neuroses born of loneliness, the cult of youth and the cultivation of the body conjoined with the neglect of the old and the infirm, and the commoditization of sex, the mediatic manipulation of consciousness, the replacing of wisdom by information, the mushrooming of pseudo-religious, messianic sects, and the ecological devastation brought about by the consumerist pursuit of science and technology.[9]

Such being the case, the only way open before us is to return to origins. Religions are like rivers whose waters are purest at their source, but as they wind their way through towns and villages finally to merge with the sea, they become more and more polluted. The Ungod is the end-result of a long history of culture-conditioned, distorted interpretations. Hence the need to peel off the successive layers of interpretations in order to arrive at Jesus' original encounter with the Divine. In fact, this is what liberation theology in Latin America and Asia has attempted to do with varying degrees of success. The deconstruction of the Ungod and the recovery of Jesus' original encounter with the Divine is indeed highly rewarding both in terms of realizing one's spiritual freedom and promoting the liberation of peoples. For the original life and message of Jesus is much more relevant to contemporary humans, particularly in the less industrialized countries, than subsequent cultic-dogmatic-legal overgrowths. But working through the maze of interpretations to their origins is an arduous task beyond the competence of the average believer. Besides, the original encounter with the Divine, being itself historically conditioned, has its own limitations. Hence the founders of religions, whether Jesus, the Buddha or the ancient Indian seers, can be for us no more than penultimate sources. For a truly new beginning in which to anchor our existence, we need the Ultimate Source that is unmediated and unconditional. And that can only be our encounter with the Divine in the here and now of history.

The simple claim that the Divine is alive and speaks to such as have ears to hear will be found disturbingly subversive by the legatees of power. For they had quarantined the Divine in the heaven above and in the tabernacle below, with the keys of both tucked away safe in clerical pockets. In the process they rendered the world a wasteland without the breath of the Divine to quicken it. Which, in turn, legitimized the institution of a hierarchy of mediators to take the Divine down to the hapless masses. Clearly, then, certain forms of religion need the carcass of the Divine to batten themselves on. Therefore, the challenge that faces us at this millennial juncture is to shift the focus of religiosity from the quarantined Divine to the Divine that is *at large* and beckons to us in the saving present. But in order to be able to perceive the presence of the Divine, we need to carry out a certain deconstruction of our own religious selves. We must divest ourselves of certain deeply ingrained conceptions which act as blinkers obstructing the vision of truth. Following the *via negativae*, the way also of the 'not thus, not thus' (*neti, neti*) of the Indian tradition, we must criticize our tendency to think of the Divine as *above* humans and nature, as *spirit* antipodal to matter, as transcending the universe of the many and the mutable, and as Father and Maker of all.

But how in this world does Divine presence itself to us? As gift and as challenge: as gift in all experiences that enable us, transport us beyond ourselves, opening out before us new frontiers of being and becoming. We meet the Divine in the soothing, enlivening, sustaining ambience of mother Earth, in the myriad ways in which she becomes word – through the whistle of the wind that blows whence and whither we know not, through the song of birds and the rustle of leaves and the perennial chant of the oceans. The Divine pulsates in that primal telluric desire (eros, *kama*, in Sanskrit) that makes the sun rise and shine and set, that makes seeds sprout, trees fruit, buds bloom, stars twinkle, and the moon turn everything it touches into gold. The Divine announces itself in the two-in-one-ness of sexual love, in the growing into, and merging with, each other of wedded existence, in friendship and the communion of shared hope and struggle, in the love that gives and in giving replenishes itself, and in the sensuous revelation of meaning that works of art are.

The self-presencing of the Divine as gift is at the same time a call addressed to us to nurture and to preserve the same gift whole and entire and to strive to realize it ever more fully, ever more intensely. Thus the self-giving of the Divine becomes enfleshed as the desire of humans for the plenitude of being. Inherent in it is also a call to share the divinely Given with one's fellow humans through word, deed and celebration.

The Divine meets us as challenge in situations where the integrity of the earth is threatened or the human is trampled upon. Here revelation assumes the form of imperatives – thou shalt not kill, thou shalt not rape, thou shalt not grind thy brother's or sister's head into dust, thou shalt not break his or her spirit or rob him or her of name and honour. Whoever is thus addressed becomes a wielder of the sword against every form of injustice and domination, a contestant, willy-nilly, of principalities and powers. Where prophecy is kindled, there also looms the inevitable foreboding of torture and death at the hands of brutalized overlords. Thus does the irruption of the Divine as challenge issue in transformative practice that humanizes the face of the earth. Seen from this angle, many are the tokens of the prophetizing breath of the Divine in the contemporary world – the emergent struggles of the deprived and the marginalized like Aborigines, Dalits, Tribals and women, and the on-going ecological and anti-nuclear movements. Significantly, none of these struggles, none of these movements was born of the initiative of the official churches. The Overgod can breed only engineers of cult, bulls and bears of religious stock exchange, not prophets of the future.

This brings us back to our point of departure. Where there is humanizing action – creative, subversive, or celebrative – there is a utopia at work, not as a blueprint for action, nor as a state of affairs to be realized once and for all, but as a receding horizon of hope and promise. As the adverse effects of middle class capitulation to corporate, neo-colonial fascism begin to be felt by the marginalized majorities of Asia and Africa,

there will definitely emerge a second wave of national liberation movements, this time aimed at recovering cultural identity and national
sovereignty. With it, the dormant utopia of the less industrialized people
will redefine itself as a new world order in which there will no longer be the
dualism of centre and periphery, of developed and developing, a world in
which there will be as many centres as there are peoples and nations, each
pursuing its own model of growth and refusing to measure themselves by
borrowed or imposed standards of development.

Groping towards a new spirituality

Implicit in the encounter with the Divine in the here and now of history is
the invitation to a new spirituality. The term spirituality is used here not in
opposition to materiality or carnality but to mean the manner in which
humans transcend themselves and reach out to the ultimate possibilities of
their existence. As such, spirituality entails both an understanding of the
deepest meaning of human existence and a commitment to realizing the
same. Seen from the vantage point of the primal source of religion which is
encounter with the Divine here and now, it is creative-subversive, telluric,
erotic-agapic, aesthetic and communitarian. In the foregoing discussion I
have already dealt with the creative-subversive character of our response to
the Divine. Here I shall do no more than offer some tentative thoughts on
the remaining characteristics that should define any relevant spirituality.

The Divine does not irrupt into our mindscape from some overworld of
disembodied spirits but appears to us enfleshed in nature, conscious and
unconscious. This calls for an up-valuation of the earth as the symbol and
abode of the Divine. It also requires that we view the earth not as an object
to be subdued but as our Mother, and ourselves as flesh become word, dust
become capable of knowing and loving. Which means that our sense of
kinship must extend beyond family, beyond humankind, to the universe of
animals and plants and planets and galaxies. Here is the basis for a *telluric*
spirituality, a spirituality instinct with a sense of reverence for, and
solidarity with, the earth, a spirituality that assumes responsibility for the
well-being of all that *is* a spirituality which sees in the earth, the dwelling of
the Divine, both the beginning and the end of the human pilgrimage.[10]

A telluric spirituality will necessarily be also *erotic*. I have spoken of the
protean desire (*kama*, eros) operating in the universe of things and
humans as a locus where we meet the Divine. It is eros that makes
everything strive after its own plenitude. It is eros that drives men and
women to seek completion through union with the other – with the other as
nature, as kin, as friend, as the person of the opposite sex, as community.

And where there is union, there is fruitfulness. More, eros is the mother of all human striving, individual as well as collective, and, as such, the driving force of history. The supreme goal of desire is mystical union with the Being of beings.

Desire being the driving force that powers the self-transcendence of the human, all genuine spirituality has to be *erotic*. But the focus of Christianity hitherto has been on 'agape', on self-giving love to the point of loving one's enemies. Agape, no doubt, represents a peak in authentic humanness, but without eros it lacks cosmic depth and human warmth, and is likely to prove impotent. Moreover, in its age-long struggle against goddess culture and fertility cult, the Judaeo-Christian tradition devalued the erotic, tended to reduce it to sexual desire, and, with St Augustine, ended up branding it a source of sin and a threat to spirituality.[11] With that came into being within the churches a political economy of guilt, based on the convertibility of the sense of guilt into money. Now, the time has come to reinstate the erotic as the source of creativity and fruitfulness and communitarian bonding. Only a spirituality that synthesizes eros and agape can face the feminist and ecological challenges of today. Finally, the new spirituality will have to be *aesthetic*. There is no self-disclosure of the Divine that is not enfleshed, be it in the processes of nature or in the events of history. Here the flesh, the materiality of revelation, is not just an external medium but, in its profoundest being, belongs to what is revealed. Revelation is, at the same time, meaning and word, truth and flesh, or – to speak in the language of goddess culture – Siva and Sakti. That is why it has already the features of art understood as the self-annunciation of meaning in sensuous form. But the self-disclosure of the Divine needs humans to give it a name and a habitat in the flux of history. And eros is what enables us to accomplish the task; for it is also the yearning for that specific plenitude of being that we call the beautiful. Eros enshrines the Divine in such wise that it abides in our midst as a thing among things, as a process among processes. This we do when we let the Divine shine forth in and through sound (music), word (poetic diction), bodily movement (dance), colour (painting) and stone (sculpture), or conjointly in all or some of these, as happens in rituals and festivals. Only by letting the Divine indwell the earth in sensuous fashion can we communicate it to our fellow humans, a task reason is ill-equipped to fulfil.

For what gives access to the Divine is not any specialized faculty like intellect or will but that innermost core of our being where feeling, thinking and living form a tensional unity. It is also the locus of aesthetic experience. Hence the indissoluble bond between art and religion. The experience of the Divine as gift and as challenge must body forth not only in the living of art but also in the art of living. We must so mould our joys and sorrows, our labour and leisure, our thinking and acting, that their sum that is life approximates to a work of art. The aesthetic must also become a structuring principle in the configuring of communities, institutions and cities so that these will radiate intimations of the Divine. More, the new spirituality must be one that sees the religious, the ethical, and the aesthetic as converging and fusing into one.

The spirituality of the future will also have to be communitarian, one that will have left behind both individualism (the fragmentation of the social) and scientific rationality (the fragmentation of consciousness). What cements the many into a community will not be money or power or reason but flesh and blood and birth and habitat, one's spontaneous longing for self-completion through the other, and the enchantment of things of beauty. And the self that longs for fullness is not the 'I' shut in upon itself but merging with the larger 'We' eros as self-seeking becomes self-giving. In this perspective, what is primary will be local communities, not wider associations based on managerial reason. This will not, however, result in the break-up of humanity into segmentary communities opposed to one another, because the local and the global converge in the oneness of the earth. For all earth is one earth. And matter, earth, is the principle not only of individuation but also of globalization, especially when viewed as indwelt by the Divine. The spirituality adumbrated here must translate itself into action aimed at rolling back the invasion of the consumerist utopia on the one hand, and realizing the socialist utopia as reinterpreted in the context of post-modernity on the other.

Notes

1. S. Kappen, *Marxian Atheism*, Madras 1983.
2. S. Kappen, *The Future of Socialism and Socialism of the Future*, Bangalore 1992.
3. Akbar S. Ahmed, *Postmodernism and Islam – Predicament and Promise*, Harmondsworth 1992.
4. Ibid.
4. Mathew Black (ed.), *Peake's Commentary on the Bible*, London 1972.
6. S. Kappen, *Jesus and Freedom*, Maryknoll, New York 1977.
7. S. Kappen, *Jesus and Cultural Revolution*, Bombay 1983.
8. S. Kappen, 'Hindutva Emergent Fascism?', in *Understanding Communalism*, Bangalore 1993.
9. Akbar S. Ahmed, *Post-modernism and Islam* (n. 3).
10. Atharva Veda, 12,1.
11. Michel Foucault, *The History of Sexuality*, Harmondsworth 1978.

Ashrams: A Movement of Spiritual Integration

Sebastian Painadath

Describing ashrams in *Concilium* in 1965 C. Murray Rogers wrote: 'These places of daring spiritual experiments and of single-eyed concentration on the interior life have given to India and to the world . . . countless souls, whose spiritual yearning has driven them insatiably to plunge into the interior mystery and to seek the ineffable Presence.'[1] During the last three decades several new ashrams of Hindu and Christian initiatives have emerged in India and in other parts of the world. Do they point to a new spiritual culture of creative inter-religious encounter, or do they represent just 'a reaction to the development theology of the West'?[2]

The ashram heritage

The word 'ashram' is derived from the Sanskrit root *a-śrama*, which means total pursuit, full dedication, 'tireless striving stretching its arms towards perfection'.[3] The four progressive stages of a person's integral growth were traditionally called ashrama: studenthood, family life, retirement into solitude and total renunciation. Gradually the sylvan resort of retirement at the third stage came to be specifically called an ashram. A few spiritual seekers spontaneously come around an enlightened person (guru) and an ashram community takes shape. The guru is acknowledged as someone who has realized the Self within and hence is capable of guiding the disciples on their path of inner pilgrimage. The pursuit of contemplation, which is the hallmark of an ashram, is expressed in the Upanishadic hymn of peace:

> May He protect us both (teacher and disciple),
> May He grant us the inner nourishment,

May we work together for spiritual power,
May the wisdom we receive be Light in us;
May there be no dislike between us

(Katha Upanishad, 1).

The guru and the disciples form a spiritual family. They live an austere life in small cottages in sylvan surroundings, possibly in a quiet valley or on the banks of a river. Clothes and food are very simple, the latter strictly vegetarian. The gate of an ashram is never to be closed. 'May the guest be God for you' (*athidhi devō bhava*) – this is the principle of ashram hospitality. Ashrams are open to spiritual seekers of any culture, religion or caste. The Upanishadic ashrams (800–300 BCE) and the Bhakti movements (800–1800 CE) were in fact a protest against the ritualism and domination of the Brahmin aristocracy. Ashrams were not introvert communities; they played a formative role in socio-political life. In them princes were initiated to martial arts, kings were given political counsel, householders received instruction on their family duties, farmers got training in agricultural skills, students learned the scriptures and methods of meditation, and young artists were initiated to music and dramatics. Above all ashrams were power-houses of spiritual renewal in society: spirituality meant harmony between the divine, the human and the cosmic dimensions of life.[4]

In course of time a tendency towards elitism grew in many ashrams and consequently they got alienated from the people. The monastic movements of Samkhya, Vedanta, later Buddhism and Jainism pushed the ashrams into isolation from the struggles of the masses. Besides, ashrams were constantly misappropriated by the religious hegemony of the Brahmins and harassed by the political machinery of the Kshatriyas and foreign invaders. Still, the idea of an ashram continued to be an elevating force in the Indian psyche, and there were always some enlightened sages and authentic ashrams which contributed a spiritual substance to the cultural evolution of the subcontinent.

From the middle of the nineteenth century a renewed interest grew in the perennial sources of India's spiritual heritage. The leaders of the Indian renaissance rediscovered the transformative power of the ashrams of ancient India. The liberative potential of contemplative pursuits and the social consequences of spiritual life came to be clearly articulated in the new ashrams which evolved in the wake of the struggle for independence. Some of the significant initiatives were the Ramakrishna Ashram of Swami Vivekananda (1897), Santiniketan of Rabindranath Tagore (1901), Aurobindo Ashram of Sri Aurobindo Ghose (1910), Satyagraha Ashram of Mahatma Gandhi (1915), Sivagiri Ashram of Narayana Guru (1912), Sevagram of Vinoba Bhave (1921) and Sivananda Ashram of Swami Sivananda (1934).

Ashrams of Christian initiative

The Christian efforts in starting ashrams began in the 1920s. The Protestant initiatives were influenced by the social ashrams of Gandhi and Tagore, while the Catholic pioneers were fascinated by the contemplative experiences of the Indian sages. The main Protestant ashrams were Christukulam (Tiruppathur) founded by Dr Jesudason and Dr Forrester Paton in 1921, Christa Prema Seva Ashram (Pune) founded by Fr Jack Winslow in 1927, and Sat Tal Ashram (Nainital) started by Stanley Jones in 1930. Their objective was effective evangelization through integral social action. On the Catholic side the first attempt to found an ashram was made by Brahmabandhab Upadhyaya in 1894; but it was thwarted by church authorities. Major initiatives began with Fr Jules Monchanin (Swami Arubi Ānandam) and Dom Henri Le Saux (Swami Abhishiktānanda), who founded Saccidānanda Ashram at Santivanam near Tiruchi in 1950, and with Fr Francis Acharya and Fr Bede Griffiths who started Kurisumala Ashram at Vagamon in Kerala in 1955. Fr Bede Griffiths moved to Santivanam in 1968 after the departure of Swami Abhishiktānanda for the Himalayas. Their major concern was inculturation of the Christian message through the pursuit of contemplation and the study of Indian spiritual classics.

From the 1960s several new ashrams were founded by native Christians who tried to integrate contemplative pursuits with social action, a concern for evangelization with inter-religious dialogue. At the National Seminar in 1969 the Indian Catholic Church officially recognized the reality of ashrams as centres of 'authentic incarnational Christian spirituality' and 'inter-religious dialogue'.[5] This gave an impetus for new Catholic initiatives. On the Protestant side a wide support for the ashram movement was already given at the World Missionary Conference, held at Tambaram, Madras in 1939. A need was felt by the Christian ashramites of various places to meet together periodically and share their experiences and problems. Thus the Protestant *Ashram Fellowship* was started in 1951, and the Catholic *Ashram Aikya* in 1978. Their meetings take place once in two years with some delegates from the other confession. Their news bulletins as well as the articles and books published during the last three decades on 'ashram theology' offer a rich material for developing contextualized theology in India.[6]

Pursuit of contemplation

By origin ashrams are an Indian phenomenon; but their contemporary theological relevance has to be seen in a global perspective. On the religious landscape of the world today there is a tension between two trends: a neurotic introversion that leads to religious fundamentalism and a groping extroversion that takes seekers beyond the confines of established religions. We could explore how the ashram culture could promote today's search for a liberative spirituality and thus provide an antidote to religious fundamentalism.

Human consciousness has a surface level of horizontal relationships and a depth dimension of vertical directedness to the Absolute. At the former level the believer cultivates an I-thou relationship with God expressed in symbols, rituals and credal forms of a particular religious heritage. But the inner call from the depth is an invitation to transcend the 'names and forms' of the Divine (*nāmarūpa*) and enter into a mystical consciousness in which the oneness between human self and divine Self is experienced. 'See the self in the Self through the Self' – this is the main theme of the Upanishads, which offer a theological basis for Indian ashram spirituality. In this relentless contemplative movement towards the all transcending and all immanent mystery of the Divine lies the real call of the ashrams. An ashram is not just a place somewhere, but a pilgrimage to the 'inner cave of the heart', a movement of the spirit in the Spirit. It designates a liberative process in which the possessive drive (*kāma*) of the ego (*aham*) is diminished and the seeker gets anchored in the integrating power (*dharma*) of the Self (*ātman*). The darkness of ignorance (*avidya*) is removed through the shining forth of the inner divine light (*jyoti*), in the intuitive faculty of perception (*buddhi*). For this transforming process the Indian masters propose the following elements, which are essentially ashram values: discernment of truth from falsehood (*vivēka*), determination to pursue the truth (*vairāgya*), equanimity (*śama*), control of senses (*dama*), renunciation (*uparati*), self-discipline (*titīksha*), integral faith in the Divine (*śradha*), serenity of the mind (*samādhana*), and an intense desire for liberation (*mumukshutva*); through them life is endowed with self-restraint (*dama*), generosity (*dāna*) and compassion (*dayā*).[7]

The one who perceives the divine Self within sees the same Self in all things. The entire realm of reality is seen as 'permeated by the Divine', as the milieu in which God is at work bringing about universal integration (*dharma*). The contemplative is motivated to participate in this divine work, by 'promoting the integral welfare of the world'.[8] For an ashramite life evolves with a two-fold dynamics: contemplative introspection (*sādhana*) and active commitment to the world (*yajna*). The Bhagavad Gita offers a spirituality of ashram life in terms of the three-fold way of integration: perception of the divine dimension of reality (*jnāna*), experience of divine love in self-surrender (*bhakti*) and active participation in the divine work in the world (*karma*). This contemplative thrust of the ashram heritage is of great significance for Christian spirituality today.[9] Over the centuries there has been a one-sided emphasis in the church on experiencing God as object, and consequently on rituals, dogmas and structures. God cannot just be an object in religious consciousness if he is not at the same time the *subject* too. In fact the Divine is to be experienced beyond the duality of the I-thou structure of the human mind. Just as (*kathos*) Jesus experienced the Father as the true *subject* of his being, we have to experience God as the true *subject* of our being (John 6.57; 15.10; 17.11,21). Authentic Christian spirituality demands the awareness of the divinization (*theopoiesis*) that is taking place deep within us (Rom. 8. 14–17; Gal. 4.6–7). A revitalization of the mystical element of spirituality is an epochal need in the church today, and for this the ashram heritage offers very valuable insights. 'The ashram is a leaven, inconspicuous, feeble, but essential, and called to bear witness to the mystery of Christ, hidden in the heart, and those in the ashram are called to awaken the Church to this mystery. All activity of mind and body will come from this Silence, the silence of the Father, and return to the Silence.'[10]

Taking inspiration from the mystical traditions of India, all ashrams of Christian initiative promote the pursuits of inner silence: initiation to contemplative prayer (*sādhana*), practice of yoga, meditative chanting (*bhajan*), offering of light (*ārati*), twilight prayer sessions (*sandhya*), celebration of the Eucharist with Indian rituals (*pūja*), sharing of spiritual experiences (*satsang*) and the study of Hindu and Christian spiritual classics.

Social transformation

These spiritual practices of Christian ashrams have met with severe criticism from two sides: conservative Christians find in the ashram movement a betrayal of Christian faith, which, according to them, can be preserved in India only by maintaining the traditional Western forms of language, symbols, dress, theology and institutionalized apostolate; social activists criticize the Christian ashrams for their insensitivity to the atrocities committed to the weaker sections of India society like women, tribals, outcasts and dalits. Theologians find that the ashrams remain at the 'micro-ethical level' of perception and hence 'lack the full perspective' to be able to 'see the structural greed of systems and institutions'.[11] If ashrams really lose the perspective of creative social concern they have no relevance in a country like India, where acute social discrimination and economic exploitation exist.

A culture of contemplation, as we have seen above, is the characteristic feature of ashram life. But one has to ask: to what experience of God does contemplation lead? A Christian ashramite would experience God's face turned towards humanity primarily and decisively on the face of the crucified and risen Christ. On the Cross the Divine was manifest as the God-with-us (Emmanuel) in our sufferings. The crucified Christ is the revelation of the woundedness of God. As long as children die of hunger and women are persecuted, tribals are exploited and dalits are marginalized, as long as tears wet this earth and innocent blood stains the ground, we can only contemplate God as a suffering God, for God is love and love is vulnerable (Matt. 25.35–36). Christian contemplation would then mean the perception of the suffering of God in suffering sisters and brothers. But suffering alone does not give meaning to life. In the resurrection of Christ the Divine was manifest as the God-with-us in our creative endeavours. The risen Christ is the revelation of the recreating power of God's love. Everything is being restored in the Divine, and ultimately 'God will be all in all' (I Cor. 15.28). The Spirit of the risen Christ is at work in our struggles for justice and in the movements for human rights, in the service of healing and in the concern to protect the environment. Christian contemplation would mean alertness to the creative urges of the Spirit in the humanizing endeavours in society.

The contemplation to be promoted in the Christian ashrams is not just a mystical immersion into the abysmal depth of being, but an awakening of consciousness to the perception of our history as God's history, an alertness to the divine Spirit that speaks to us constantly through the problems and struggles of our times.[12] Then the gnosis (*jana*) of contemplation would evolve into agape (*bhakti*) of liberative action (*karma*). Then ashram would become 'a place where what is broken is made whole, what is diverse in the spirit is integrated and the oneness of the self with the whole of reality is achieved'.[13] In fact some of the great social and spiritual liberation movements in India emerged out of ashrams. The most conspicuous of them is the Independence Movement that was spiritually enlivened by the Satyagraha ashram of Mahatma Gandhi. He perceived that in India no socio-political project would transform people unless it is supported by an integrated spirituality. The tragedy today is that this vision of Gandhi has been forgotten, and consequently social projects and political actions have become exploitative to a great extent.

Christian ashrams can play an important role in promoting a spirituality of integrative contemplation and liberative action. From such an ashram culture social activists working at grass-roots level would take a lot of strength and inspiration. An ashram community with its values of freedom, simplicity, equality, hospitality and sharing would embody that community of counter-culture which the justice movements want to create. This would then become a centre where training is given in values, ideals, motivations and methods for those who commit themselves to the creation of a new humanity. Integral formation has always been a traditional function of ashrams in Indian society. Individuals and teams of liberative praxis do need an integrated spirituality and a holistic vision of reality; ashrams would offer them the spiritual perspectives they need. An ashram could be a centre of spiritual recharging for an activist.[14] For the theologians, who often live quite insulated from the struggles of the poor, ashrams could be places where life in evangelical simplicity and closeness to people is made possible; only from such a life of insertion can creative theological reflection evolve with power and credibility in India. Consequently ashrams would offer the suitable *seed-bed* for the formation of future priests and religious.

The integration of contemplation (*jnana*), devotion (*bhakti*) and liberative action (*karma*) seems to emerge as the spiritual objective of the Christian ashrams in India today, though each ashram has a thrust of its own.[15] All ashrams offer an atmosphere of silence and generously welcome seekers for reflection and retreat. Saccidānanda Ashram (Tiruchi), Anjali Ashram (Mysore), Jeevandhāra Ashram (Jaiharikal), Sameeksha (Kalady) and Jaganmātha Ashram (Tiruchi) offer courses in integrated Indian spirituality and initiation to Indian methods of meditation. A good library with the classics of spirituality is at the disposal of students and seekers in these centres. Prayer sessions with Indian devotional forms are conducted regularly at Jeevandhāra Ashram, Anjali Ashram, Kurisumula Ashram (Vagamon), Sāntisadan (Kothamangalam), and Ānmodaya Ashram (Kancheepuram). Creative experiments in developing an Indian form of eucharistic celebration too are being made in some of these places. All ashrams are somehow involved in the life of the local people. Christukula Ashram (Tiruppathur), Christian Medical Fellowship Ashram (Oddanchatram), Christa Panthi Ashram (Sihora) and Bethany Ashram (Trivandrum) run hospitals attached to them; the medical staff lives an ashram life from which they draw spiritual nourishment for caring the sick. Christavashram (Manganam) Bethel Ashram (Tiruvalla) and Tapōvan (Katyawar) conduct schools for destitute children. The Ashram of the Little Brothers of Jesus (Tiruvannamalai) takes care of the leprosy patients in forty-five villages. Tirumalai Ashram (Nagercoil), Anpu Vazhvu Ashram (Palani), Sat Tal Ashram (Nainital) and Saccidānanda Ashram (Tiruchi) have developmental projects in the neighbouring villages. Christa Prema Seva Ashram (Pune) is involved in conscientization programmes for women. This rich variety of services shows that the Christian ashrams do play a liberative role in society. What is needed today is for them to articulate a critique on the oppressive elements of religiosity and get more associated with peoples' movements for justice, human rights and protection of the environment, without sacrificing their spiritual identity. It is here that a creative collaboration between ashramites and social activists is called for. That would give rise to new *social* ashrams like the 'village ashram', 'tribal ashram' and 'dalit ashram'.

A pilgrim community in the church

Relationship with ecclesiastical authority is a question that is vexing many Christian ashrams today. In general the Protestant ashrams have more autonomy than the Catholic ashrams, which are mostly started by priests and religious. Bishops and religious superiors tend to consider the ashrams as ecclesiastical institutions under their jurisdiction. 'As a matter of fact, if we respect the nature, identity and uniqueness of an ashram as an Indian reality or experience, it is outside all legal and institutional framework.'[16] At the basis of this problem there is the age-old and essential tension which exists between charisma and authority within the church.

In so far as Christian ashramites take inspiration from the heritage of Christian faith, a sense of belonging to the believing community and a certain accountability to its spiritual leaders is necessary. This is a safeguard against infantile forms of personality cult and uncritical submission to a 'guru' in an ashram.[17] However, an ashram is an open community of seekers guided by the Spirit, and hence the charismatic freedom for them to respond creatively to the Spirit must be recognized in the Church.[18] Structural restrictions should not block their search for the Divine, and juridical demands should not stifle the Spirit, 'which blows where it wills'. 'An ashram is to go beyond organized religion and this is its reason for being. We must distinguish between the institutional Church and the eschatological Church. The ashram, because it has no juridical status in the institutional Church, does not come under Canon Law.'[19] Ashrams would embody the basileic community that the church is called to become, and hence point to the direction the future church may take. From the spiritual culture of an ashram, the church can imbibe the values of authenticity, simplicity and mobility, which are genuine values of the kingdom of God. An ashram community that is normally centred upon a spiritual master (guru) constantly reminds the hierarchical church that authenticity in exercising authority comes not just through ordination or appointment, but out of a deep spiritual experience. Ministers in the church can gain credibility in witnessing to the gospel only if their life is shaped by simplicity and generosity which are embodied in the ashram way of life. There is a tendency in the church to institutionalize everything in order to safeguard stability and continuity; ashrams on the other hand are pilgrim communities which are characterized by mobility in response to the call of the Spirit. Over the centuries there has been the blossoming of new forms of consecrated life in the church; ashrams point to the emergence of charismatic inter-denominational, inter-faith communities at the threshold of the third millenium. What is needed is radical openness to 'listen to what the Spirit is saying to the church' (Rev. 2.7).

Inter-religious fellowship

Christian ashrams are in general well received by the Hindus in India; however, a certain suspicion has been expressed in some Hindu circles today. It has been asked whether the Christian ashrams form the new missionary strategy in establishing 'institutions to brainwash and convert India's unwary masses'. The deeper theological question is also raised: with what moral right can Christians found ashrams when they 'continue to claim a divine monopoly on salvation'?[20] In today's context of the upsurge of fundamentalism and the politicization of religiosity, Christian ashrams are challenged to reflect on their basic premises. Ashram is a community in relentless pursuit of the Transcendent, and hence a transreligious community of seekers. However, every ashram lives on the heritage of the spiritual experience of a guru. An ashram of Christian inspiration would consider Jesus Christ as the true guru (satguru).[21] This does not mean that Christ is to be projected just as *an object* of worship within the frame of a particular religion. True worship takes place 'in spirit and truth' (John 4.24). The divine Spirit revealed in Christ leads the seeker to the 'depths of God' (I Cor. 2.10), to 'oneness with God' (John 17.23), into the experience of 'being filled with all the fullness of God' (Eph.3.19) and to communion with all (John 15.17). In this Spirit-guided process of transformation all ashramites – seekers from all religious traditions – find themselves as co-pilgrims marching towards one goal. 'We are pilgrims of the Absolute.'[22] It is a pilgrimage in contemplative silence into the 'cave of the heart' and in active collaboration into the areas of social liberation. In the process of this pilgrimage each one shares with others his or her deepest experiences and motives, and is in turn enriched by others.

For this creative inter-religious dialogue the ashram offers a conducive place. 'An ashram helps first to *be* before saying or doing.'[23] An ashram is by nature a 'transreligious community', and hence a 'multireligious community'. The contemplative atmosphere, closeness to people, harmony with nature, simplicity of life, generous hospitality and above all the spiritual fellowship among seekers create a room suited for promoting a culture of dialogue among believers of various religions. Some attempts in this direction are actually being made in the Christian ashrams today. At Aikya Ālayam (Madras) and Christa Prema Seva Ashram (Pune) regular sessions of inter-religious dialogue and prayer are conducted. Saccidānanda Ashram (Tiruchi), Snēhasadan (Pune) and Sameeksha (Kalady) organize seminars on inter-religious questions of theology. An experiment in the theological formation of future priests in an ashram context is being made at Matridham Ashram (Varanasi) and Sameeksha (Kalady). At Art Ashram (Bangalore), Gnyan Prakāsh Ashram (Bombay) and Ishālayam (Madras) creative experiments are being made in the areas of Indian Christian art, music and dance. Christian ashrams everywhere take initiatives to organize common celebration of important festivals of all religious communities. Christian ashramites have to collaborate more intensely with believers of other religions 'in the task of bettering this world where all live together', in the projects of the promotion of justice, human rights and harmony.[24]

Ashrams point to a new direction in the spiritual evolution of humanity. The religious person of the future will be an *inter*-religious person. This does not mean that one has one's feet in two boats, but that the spiritual seeker will be deeply rooted in the core experience of his or her own faith, and at the same time honestly open to the faith of the other, in view of being challenged and enriched by the other. God is greater than all religions, greater than our hearts. Scriptures and symbols – *Deus semper major*: this would be the basic message of an ashram. Holistic and integral liberation of the human person in harmony with the environment would be the central concern of an ashram. The creative programme of an ashram would be to discover the unity of the convergent movements of a humanizing spirituality deep within the diversities of religions and secular ideologies. Ashrams of the future will be sacramental communities of the spiritual unity of humanity.

Notes

1. C. Murray Rogers, 'Hindu Ashram Heritage: God's Gift to the Church', *Concilium* 1, 1965, 73.
2. EATWOT (Ecumenical Association of Third World Theologians) Statement, 1981, article 58, *Vidyajyoti* 46, 1982, 92.
3. R. Tagore, *Gitanjali*, poem 35.
4. Vedanta Kesari, 'Evolution of Monastic Ideal in Hinduism', in Ramakrishna Math (ed.), *Monasticism Ideal and Traditions*, Madras 1991, 81–147.
5. Catholic Bishops' Conference of India (ed.), *Church in India Today*, Bangalore 1970, 243, 259, 343.
6. For a good bibliography on ashram, cf. E. Pulsfort, *Christliche Ashrams in Indien*, Altenberge 1989, 219–34.
7. Vivekachudamani, 17–30; Brihadaranyaka Upanishad, 5, 2.
8. Bhagavad Gita, 9.4; 6.29–31; 3.25; 12.4.
9. S. Painadath, 'Die Bhagavad Gita und christliche Spiritualität', in Peter Schreiner, *Bhagavad Gita*, Zürich 1991, 189–223; S. Painadath, 'Mukti, the Hindu Notion of Liberation', in D. Cohn-Sherbok (ed.), *World Religions and Human Liberation*, Maryknoll 1992, 66–77.
10. B. Griffiths, 'The Ashram as a Way of Transcendence', in Vandana (ed.) *Christian Ashrams, A Movement with a Future?*, Delhi 1993, 31.
11. EATWOT Statement (n. 2); G. Soares Prabhu, 'Letter on Ashrams', in Vandana, *Christian Ashrams* (n. 10), 153–6.
12. S. Painadath, 'Contemplation and Liberative Action', *Vidyajyoti* 52, 1988, 10–223.
13. C. D'Souza, 'Ashrams and the Socio-Economic and Political Needs of India', in Vandana, *Christian Ashrams* (n. 10), 93.
14. M. Amaldoss, 'Ashrams and Social Justice', *Word and Worship* 15, 1982, 205–214; Vandana, *Social Justice and Ashrams*, Bangalore 1982, 16–53.
15. For details about Christian ashrams, cf. H. Ralston, *Christian Ashrams. A New Religious Movement in Contemporary India*, Queenston 1987, 69–110.
16. D. S. Amalorpavadas, 'Ashram Aikya: Whence and Whither?', *Word and Worship*, 17, 1984, 343; M. Kämpchen, 'Ashrams – Stätte religiöser Gemeinschaft', *Geist und Leben*, 55, 1982, 284.
17. C. Cornille, *The Guru in Indian Catholicism*, Louvain 1991, 198.
18. W. Taylor, *Acknowledging the Lordship of Christ*, Delhi 1992, 40–51.
19. B. Griffiths, 'Hindu Ashram Heritage' (n. 1), 30, 32.
20. S. R. Goel, *Catholic Ashrams*, New Delhi 1988, 3, 14.
21. Ashram Aikya Statement, 1978.
22. Pope John Paul II at New Delhi, February 1986 (*Pope Speaks to India*, Bombay 1986, 22).
23. M. Lederle, 'Ashrams and Dialogue', *Word and Worship* 17, 1984, 110.
24. Pope John Paul II to the Leaders of Non-Christian Religions, Madras, February 1986 (*Pope Speaks to India* [n. 22], 84).

Mysticism: Flight from the World or Responsibility for the World?

Willigis Jäger

Who am I?

Evolution has equipped the human species with possibilities of knowledge and behaviour by virtue of which it can to some degree find its way around and assert itself in the biosphere of this planet. At first human beings were denied the possibility of grasping the nature of Being itself directly. Nor did they need to during the years when humankind was in its infancy. At first it was enough for the survival of the species to find food and procreate, to be able to be afraid and if need be to run away, to have a mode of understanding and to be capable of the feelings of attraction and repulsion. Later, human beings developed projections on an omnipotent creative being, in order to interpret their own existence and that of the world. No more than this was needed for survival.

Today, however, it is no longer possible for human beings to bracket off the sphere of universal consciousness from their humanity. Given the dead end in which the development of humanity now finds itself, it is no longer enough to take over unquestioningly our ancestors' religious interpretation of the world. Evidently only a quest for new paradigms and a quantum leap to a new level of consciousness can save us from disaster.

According to Jean Gebser,[1] human consciousness developed from an archaic pre-consciousness into a magical consciousness, from a magical consciousness into a mythical consciousness, and from a mythical consciousness into a mental consciousness. Today human beings evidently face a renewed opening of their consciousness, in the direction of the transpersonal and the mystical. To adapt a saying of Karl Rahner's, in the future not only Christians but also all human beings will either be mystics of they just will not be.

However, the development is not equal everywhere. Whereas part of humankind knows that in the last centuries it has allowed itself to be deceived by the worst superstition in its history, by intellectualism, materialism and positivism, the other part is getting more and more deeply entangled in it. However, those who are open cannot do other than seek new interpretations in order to illuminate for others the meaning of their existence.

Who am I? In our day this age-old question is being raised again with new existential acuteness, indeed with desperation. Why do we run round this utterly insignificant speck in the cosmos for a few decades? What are our sixty, seventy or eighty years of life in the face of the billions of years of cosmic happening? We now know that if we condense the eighteen to twenty billion years for which the cosmos has existed into the space of a year, the human species first emerged on 31 December, five minutes before midnight, and Jesus Christ was born fifteen seconds before the end of the year. We also know that 98% of all species on this earth have died out. Possibly the human species, too, will suffer the same fate. But the primary reality which we in the Christian West call God will go on existing after the death of every individual, and even after the extinction of the human species in billions of forms.

Against these cosmic dimensions the question arises of the meaning of the individual's life and a new interpretation of religious terms like 'resurrection' and 'redemption'. The meaning of being human cannot be fulfilled in its personal structure, but only in experience of and identification with that primal reality, with life itself, which arises in constantly new forms.

The new view of humankind

The new view of humankind is based on a new cartography of the human psyche. In it, the personal element forms only a small part, whereas for the traditional interpretation and view of human beings and the world it represents the sole basis. For example, in its excessive stress on the personal, traditional theology reveres an almost unsurpassable geocentrism and homocentrism. We suffer from the vain illusion that we stand at the centre.

In reality evolution is not centred at all on the earth or even on the human person, but in cosmic dimensions. The universe can get by without the human species, and we are certainly not the only beings aware of our existence.

Finding meaning means experiencing behind all structures that dimension from which everything comes. This is possible if we venture the leap from personal to transpersonal consciousness. In transpersonal psychology this transpersonal consciousness is further divided into fine consciousness, causal consciousness and cosmic consciousness.[2] The last of these is the level of mysticism. And the overpowering experience of the mysticism of the East and West is that the primal reality manifests life, divinity, the numinous – or whatever else one may care to call it – in every structure, and therefore also in this our human structure.

Before I return to the cosmic consciousness, just a few thoughts on the crisis in which religion generally is caught up today. Here I am in part following the remarks by Ken Wilber in his book *Der glaubende Mensch*.

Crisis of religion

Religion always gets into a crisis when the predominant interpretation of the world is put into question by the experience of a higher level. Nowadays it is the mystical level which more than ever puts in question the theistic religions which build on cognitive knowledge. More and more, human beings stand on the threshold of a transpersonal experience. They have an inkling, and indeed not a few even experience, that there is a certainty which transcends the purely cognitive truths of faith.

Above all in the theistic religions we confront a vertical change, a transformation, as Ken Wilber calls it: 'The present translation (an attempt at renewal within the system, reformation) is beginning no longer to be able to perform its soothing, phase-specific, integrative tasks; in other words its units of meaning no longer dominate everyday understanding; too many of its symbols of immortality (in Christianity e.g. belief in the resurrection, notions of redemption, images of God) have suffered shocking damage; structural tensions are gradually increasing and driving the system into unrest and confusion; the structure is finally beginning to loosen and crumble. If there are no seed-crystals capable of life, either the system regresses to lower forms (as is happening today) or collapses completely; if there are seed-crystals capable of life, then the structural tensions are absorbed and channelled through the crystals, and through its conflict the system as a whole arrives at a higher level of structural organization and integration. The old translation dies out; there is a transformation; new and higher translations are born.'[3]

Thus the change in religious consciousness or the transformation of religion is a leap from one level to another. Whereas the old translation can be compared with moving furniture around on the same floor, the transformation is like moving to another floor.

The increasing need for a universal-mystical crossing of the frontier of the self results from a longing for meaning in life, for totality and consummation, and results in a universal religious feeling. It leads to what the *philosophia perennis* understands as the transcendent unity of all religions. Any mystical way is a way out of the narrow confessional understanding of religion. That need not mean a farewell to religion in itself, but mysticism bursts apart and transcends everything that religion seeks to reify and prescribe. Religion is only a map to show the way into mystical experience. However, unfortunately religion in general only teaches its adherents to travel with their fingers on the map instead of allowing them to make their own way through the landscape. Here Eastern religions can be as superficial and sterile as Christianity, unless both are constantly given new life by mystical experience.

Transformation of religion – not just reformation

What we need is a radically new interpretation of Christian faith in the sense of a transformation. It would be good here to be able to go by the insights of contemporary science. For example, we experience our bodies as firm and tangible. But in reality – so science tells us – they are as empty as interstellar space. Our bodies are like solar systems in which there is empty space between the individual heavenly bodies. But emptiness is not nothingness. It is the wealth of non-material consciousness. The non-material consciousness is timeless and spaceless, but it constantly expresses itself in time and space, in a material body. We are not lumps of human flesh which move through time and space separately from one another; we are immaterial and timeless consciousness which has limited itself in a body, experiences itself in it and will pass away again as this body. The great world theatre is played out act by act in the constant coming and going of all forms and structures.

Every form strives for the experience of the unity of life, for the transcending of its individuality. Only in the experience of the life which underlies all things do human beings receive a meaningful interpretation of their individual existence. All other interpretations can be destroyed with rational argument. Religion should help us to experience this life. That is its prime task. Its doctrinal structure should serve this task alone. But unfortunately a developed religion all too easily becomes fixed as an end in itself.

Because dogmas and morality as proclaimed today no longer correspond to the reality of human experience, many people are leaving the institution and seeking a new foundation for their lives. Not a few have followed esoteric paths which can be found in all religions but which are not taught by all religions.

Ways like Zen, Yoga, Vipassana and contemplation are spiritual, less religious ways in the usual sense of the word; for they have to do with experience and not with prescribed contents of faith. Very similar to one another in their basic structure, they are part of a *philosophia perennis* of a kind that has a foundation in our humanity and can be demonstrated in all religions, cultures and times. Here is to be found the real access to universal reality and the beginnings of a cosmic religion. But first of all – as has really always been the case – this can only be based on heretics, holy fools, sages and nonconformists. It will be some time yet before the human species can understand itself as a time-conditioned and transitory species of God.

Cosmic religion

In cosmic religion, human beings know themselves to be bound up with the universe and with everything, and to be one. Here the new view of the universe since the development of science largely coincides with the basic ideas of the spiritual traditions of the *philosophia perennis*. This is probably precisely what Eckhart thought when he preached: 'All that you think and say about your God is more you than him; you blaspheme him, for all those wise masters in Paris cannot say what he really is. If I had a God whom I could understand, I would never want to recognize him as my God. So I keep quiet and do not chatter about him, do not adorn him with the clothes of attributes and properties, but accept him "without properties", as he is a transcendent being and a transcendent nothingness.'[4]

Cosmic religion does not know any concept of God in a personal form. 'Person' appears more and more as a prison, a prison for God as for human beings.

The great religious geniuses of all times, whose experience was later prescribed as religions, are marked by such a cosmic religious quality. They did not know any doctrinal structure or any God whom human beings have created more or less in their own image. Rather, they taught that human beings were made in the image of God, i.e. that this universal life manifested itself as human form in the most varied way and in human beings. 'God is in you. You are his sons and daughters.' That was the primal experience of Jesus and all the wise men of this earth. And they simply wanted to show human beings a way to this experience of God. Like Jesus, human beings are to understand that they are from God, that they are one with the Father.

However, traditional theology is inclined to dismiss such an understanding as neo-Gnosticism. But in contrast to historical Gnosticism, which turned away from the world in contempt, the genuine mystical depth-experience leads to complete affirmation of the world and responsibility for it; for the mystic experiences all that is as a manifestation of that primal energy which in the theistic religions is called God, and in the Eastern religions Sunyata, nature, Nirvana, etc.

There are those who would like to dismiss such an experience as pantheism. But what is experienced here is not the non-duality of divine life and human form. What is non-duality? We might take a gold coin as an example. A gold coin is a unity. But in reality it consists of the material gold and the form coin. A coin is not the same as gold and gold is not the same as a coin. But the two can only appear together; they are not-two.

The symbol of the eight on its side, the symbol of infinity, is often used for this non-duality. One side corresponds to what in Zen is called emptiness or nature, the other side is the manifestation. Eckhart calls the two sides 'Godhead' and creation. The two can only appear together, and in their unity they make up the whole human being or the whole cosmos. Information passes from one side to the other, but unfortunately most people are aware only of the biological side of their existence and therefore cannot recognize and eliminate disturbances which are based on a lack of openness to the other side.

In mysticism, that unity is experienced which knows neither space nor time, which recognizes itself in all structures, knows itself to be bound up with all and therefore can say 'I' to all. Thus Al Hallaj and Jesus and some other mystics uttered statements like 'I am God', or 'I and the Father are one'. What they really meant was 'God is I': in other words, God manifests himself as this I-structure of mine; God manifests himself in any form as 'I-structure'. Any self is a self-limitation of God which is again relativized in the mystical experience of unity. In addition, as mysticism says, the self must 'die'. What we call God is revealed in a constant being born and dying to all the transitory forms and structures of this world. God is born as galaxy, as human being and angel, and passes away as galaxy, as human being and angel.

Such language is of course open to attack. Anyone who interprets differently terms which are prescribed in the internal system of theology runs the risk of being branded a heretic. Nevertheless, an old conceptuality and hermeneutic of religious texts taken over more or less uncritically is no longer of any use to people. They ask about the origin of such texts and the origin of religion generally. By contrast, unfortunately too few theologians venture the step from faith as holding what has come down to them to be true to faith from experiences. The bold ones among them encounter grateful companions, but also repudiation and hostility.

Human beings – an incarnation of God

Max Planck, who discovered quantum mechanics and Planck's quantum effect, gave a lecture in Florence in 1944 on 'The Nature of Matter'. At that time, among other things he already remarked: 'As a physicist, i.e. as someone who has devoted his whole life to the most sober science, namely the investigation of matter, I can hardly be regarded as an enthusiast, so I say to you after my investigations of the atom: there is no such thing as matter in itself. All matter comes into being and exists only through its own power, which sets the atomic particles in motion and holds them together in the tiniest solar system of the atom . . . So we must certainly assume a deliberate intelligent Spirit behind this power. This Spirit is the primal ground of all matter. What is real and true is not visible but transitory matter, but the invisible, immortal Spirit! Now as there similarly cannot be Spirit in itself but every spirit belongs to a being, we are compelled to accept spiritual beings.'[5]

The whole universe is none other than the correspondence between the two poles of individuality and totality, matter and Spirit, or – to put it in Christian terms – creation and God, the manifestation Son and the primal principle Father. We are part of an infinite fluctuation of the universe. There is no outside mover. There is only this flow of timeless energy which constantly keeps structuring itself.

Here mysticism has to avoid two extremes above all: an excessive stress on the individual and a dissolution into the One and Only. As human beings we are quite individual structures of the primal principle, irreplaceable and unique. We are the individual steps in God's dance. We are the individual notes in God's symphony. God has not composed this symphony in order to perform it constantly now. It resounds as this timeless symphony. It resounds as this totally individual structure of my person. It resounds in a unique way in each individual thing. It keeps resounding here and in this moment as space and time.

Being human does not mean having a material body which has developed spirit, but being non-material divine consciousness which has created this individual human structure. The cosmos is intelligent (divine) energy which manifests itself in the most different structures and thus also in human beings.

In Christian terms this means that we are divine life which has this experience as human beings. And therefore in our deepest being we find ourselves one with the whole cosmos: hence the statement 'I am that'. I am not divided. I am the accomplishment of this stream of the energy of divine life. The message of the incarnation of Jesus wants to proclaim to us nothing other than the fact that we are divine life which has incarnated itself. As in Jesus, the divine principle has also become human in us. And the universe is none other than the ongoing materialization of this divine field of consciousness. God creates himself at every moment.

The way to mystical experience

The way to this mystical experience is age-old, and the basic structure of all esoteric ways is more or less equal. They lead through the evacuation of consciousness or the unification of consciousness. The evacuation of consciousness means that one gives pure attention to everything that emerges in the consciousness (ideas, feelings, images) without judging it or condemning it. One denies nothing, rejects nothing, regards everything with the attitude of a bystander and then lets it go. Here the attitude of the witness plays an important role. Gradually practice leads to the insight that everything that is played out in our consciousness is nothing but a series of changing and fleeting sensations, and that our self therefore has neither substance or reality. Slowly in the course of practice identification with the self disappears. I am only a neutral onlooker and witnesses of the passing scene, no longer an agent in it.

But it is not yet enough simply to be a witness; for there are always two elements: the witness and what is perceived. Therefore the direction of the second way aims at a unification of consciousness. I fix my attention on one thing, on my breath, a sound, a word, until I, the one who is breathing, am no longer there but the breath is; however, only this one breath: nothing before it and nothing after it. This unification of consciousness, which has been practised for a long time, aims at unity with all being.

Whatever practice one adopts, the individual always experiences the transition to the level of the experience of unity as a dying. The mystics of both East and West therefore speak of the death of the self as the presupposition for change. As soon as there is a threat that the self will lose its domination, it will be seized with anxiety and react with constantly new defensive measures. But with increasing practice they no longer protect it. Uncertainty, confusion and anxiety increase. Finally there is a collapse. This collapse is the presupposition for any authentic transformation. The way to the real transformation of the personality leads through the wilderness, through solitude, frustration, despair and the death of the self. But that is too dramatic a process for everyone to venture to take upon themselves. So many people arrive at the recognition of the deepest goal of their life very late, if at all. Some find a spiritual director helpful. Recently in an increasing number of countries so-called Spiritual Emergence Networks have been appearing, groups in which social workers, therapists and spiritual directors come together to help men and women in a spiritual crisis.

Mysticism – regression or fulfilment?

The negation of the world and life has always been a danger, especially in Christian mysticism; for there is a great temptation to feel this body and this life a burden and a limitation and to escape into a false selflessness. But authentic mysticism does not flee from what is into the uroboric unity of the state of paradise. On the contrary, we are confronted with the wealth of humanity. Humankind as a whole has to take this way into adulthood and free itself from the arms of the Great Mother.[5] Mystics can become pioneers on this way. Whereas uroboric pseudo-mysticism denies, indeed despises, the world, true mysticism affirms not only the world and human beings, but also the self and the process of history in time. Indeed mystics experience everything as a form of expression of the primal reality. Their cosmic consciousness does not make them wait for a future in the beyond, for a heaven. Rather, consummation comes in the here and now. It is only hidden. If human beings have overcome their almost childish homo-centricity and geocentricity, they know that they are involved in an evolutionary process in which the divine unfolds. In that case the *visio beatifica* (the blessed vision) means experiencing all being born and dying, the good and also what is called evil, as the accomplishment of the life of God in the here and now. In everything the creative power of the divine overflows. God 'truly reveals himself and consummates himself entirely as he is, and so fills human beings to overflowing that they spill out and overflow as the superabundant fullness of God'.[6] Therefore the mystic also speaks of the 'sacrament of the moment'. So in his book *Self-Abandonment to Divine Providence*, Jean-Pierre de Caussade can write: '"Truly," said Jacob, "God is in this place and I knew it not." You are seeking God, dear soul, and he is everywhere, everything cries his name to you, everything gives him to you, he is at your side, around you, within you, and astride your path; he remains with you and you still seek him! . . . Ah, you are seeking the idea of God, while you possess his substance, you are pursuing perfection and it is there all the while in everything that comes to meet you. Your sufferings, your actions, your inclinations are, as it were, the sacramental species under which God gives himself to you, while you are off chasing your sublime ideas. But God will not come to your house clothed in their splendour.'[7] It is from this experience that the mystic's affirmation of the world, responsibility for the world and creativity derive.

The mystic's responsibility for the earth

The conviction that mysticism and social commitment are incompatible comes above all from the camp of the Christian mystics. Their aversion from the world is closely connected with a wrong interpretation of the so-called Fall. What we usually call original sin, namely the knowledge of good and evil, is not sin, apostasy from God, but a necessary step in human development from the paradisal state of symbiosis to a stronger individuality.

A false mysticism cannot accept the abyss in God. It is unwilling to perceive that life is polarized, in a tension which also includes the devil, evil, guilt, sin and death. So it says that the world and human beings are fallen, guilty, perverse and corrupt. In the end false mysticism regards creation as a divine error or the work of a second-rate demiurge and turns away from it.

By contrast, an authentic mystical experience on the one hand transcends any confessional intolerance and on the other is quite naturally the source of responsible action in the world. Here it needs no moral precepts – 'you shall', 'you must' – of the kind given out in religion. Rather, 'the deeper the experience, the greater the mercy'.

Harada Dai un Sogaku Roshu, the Father of the Zen direction to which I belong, reports the following encounter which he had at the age of seven with his Dharma brother Kato Chodo: 'One morning he (Kato Chodo) discovered a chopstick in the garbage. He brought it in and called me. He showed me the chopstick and said, "What is that?" "A chopstick," I replied. "Yes, it's a chopstick. Is it useless?" "No!" I said, "it can still be used." "Yes," he said, "but I found it in the garbage among some other useless things. You have killed this chopstick. Perhaps you know the proverb: anyone who kills another digs two graves. You have killed this chopstick; it will kill you."' 'From then on,' said Harada, 'I was very careful about everything.'

What does this tell us? Everything is a form of expression of the divine. That we live separated from everything is an illusion, but it is an illusion which kills us. Everything is woven into our own existence. What we do to others we do to ourselves. The mystical way runs through the midst of our everyday life. The mystery can take place just as well in the railway station as in the church.

Yet we still keep waiting for the great redeemer from outside: someone will do it for us; we need only hang on to his hem. However, true religious leaders do not want to redeem. Rather, they have called to conversion, to turn inwards, to the essential, to our divine nature. But human beings have preferred to erect altars to religious leaders and ask them instead to perform on themselves the metanoia that they have lived out; for the way of transformation is long and difficult. A fundamental transformation of the world will never come about from a new social system but only from the conversion of the individual.

Mysticism – does it bring harmony or revolution?

The mystic often belongs to a religion but need not necessarily belong to a confession. The mystics attached to a confession are certainly the best known, but they are not necessarily the most significant. Mystics who do not belong to any religion can express themselves much more freely. Anyone who was tied to a confession came into conflict with the fixed dogmas in a particular religion (and still does today); for as Neumann has shown, the mystical experience cannot be other than anti-conventional, anti-collective and anti-dogmatic, because it is a new experience of the numinous. Mysticism is always revolutionary, and is therefore felt by the institution to be disruptive, if not heretical. Many mystics are attacked and condemned, indeed executed, by the institution – or they have masked their statements in non-religious terminology, so that they have been recognized only as initiates. There is less and less recognition that mysticism is the lifegiving element of and could be the constant source of every religion.

Human beings have a future

Mystics are on the way towards experiencing themselves more and more as a whole, i.e. as a collective personality. As human beings at present we are in a state of puberty. We do not really know properly who we are. But the development of this personality of humankind is progressing with increasing speed. At least we already recognize that thinking in terms of friend and foe, nationalism, religious fanaticism, violence, etc. threaten us all, and not only in the limitable places where these problems are pressing at present. We can certainly hardly imagine how this our human future will look one day. But it is already announcing itself in a growing openness and sensitivity to mysticism. We discover that the universe is Spirit and that everything physical is merely a concentration of this Spirit.

Human beings are on the way towards being human. Despite the constant flood of bad news in the media, the divine principle will not allow itself to be hindered in its development by *homo sapiens*. The world is not the failed attempt of a second-rate demiurge but the work of God, who has confirmed to us that everything is good. Human beings have a future because they are the future of God.

Translated by John Bowden

Notes

1. J. Gebser, *Ursprung und Gegenwart*, Stuttgart 1953.
2. Cf. K. Wilber, *Der glaubende Mensch*, 40ff.
3. Ibid., 72ff.
4. F. Pfeiffer, *Meister Eckhart*, Aalen 1962, 183.
5. E. Neumann, *Kulturentwicklung und Religion*.
6. J. Quint, *Meister Eckhart*, Munich 1963, 277.
7. J.-P. de Caussade, *Self-Abandonment to Divine Providence*, London 1971, 130.

Mysticism. An Opportunity for the Renewal of the Church

Jean-Claude Sagne

'The church does not need reformers, it needs saints,' said Bernanos. If there is a real opportunity for renewal in the church, it is the birth of a holiness movement among Christians. Mystical experience can only be a sign of this, a manifestation and an unfolding of the holiness which is the reality of the love that inspires and simplifies lives.

To create a dialectical relationship between the two terms which are our concern, mysticism and the church, I shall introduce a third to mediate between them: scripture. It is by its relationship to scripture that mysticism tends to establish itself and become integrated into the life of the church. It is by its relationship to scripture that the church returns to the source of its life and can undergo a renewal. Mystical experience brings to light the life which is contained and hidden in scripture, while the role of the church is to help the reception of scripture in the fullness of its meaning. It is from within itself that mystical experience tends towards assuming a shape which sets it in the church. The church seeks among mystics an indication of the active proximity of the invisible world which is its basis and inspiration. The church is the communion of those who receive the Word of God in the obedience of faith.

Mystical experience is an encounter with God which realizes a word of scripture in life.

This article will have three parts. First, in order to justify my approach to mystical experience, I shall examine the great Carmelite reformers Teresa of Avila and John of the Cross, to illustrate the relationship between mysticism and scripture. Then, from among the wealth of contemporary spiritual quests, I shall take the case of the charismatic renewal to trace the actual transition of an experience of prayer towards forms established in all spheres. Another development will put us in a

position to denote the relationship of attraction between mystical experience and the life of the institutional church, namely the quest for
intelligible mystical experience: the transition from witness to book. The
church can only be renewed by mystical experience when this has attained
its essential simplicity, which is the blossoming of the baptismal life of
union with the three divine Persons on a basis of attention and abandonment. The specific features of a spiritual experience attract attention,
intrigue or irritate, but they do not create a school. Now the way of
simplicity is obedience to the Word of God received in scripture as the
book of life.

I. Scripture in letters of fire

Bergson said that Christian mysticism is simply scripture, but written in
letters of fire! The relationship between mystical experience and scripture
is striking in the cases of the founders of the reformed Carmel. Shortly
after her second conversion in Lent 1553, Teresa of Avila had the bitter
experience of being deprived of books of spirituality written in Castilian.
This was the consequence of a decision of the Inquisition made in 1558
proscribing books in the vernacular about the Bible or spiritual life. Teresa
received an inner word from Jesus who himself came to console her: 'Do
not be troubled, I will give you a living book.'[1] From scripture, through
contemporary witnesses, Teresa passed to Jesus, the living Word. It was
from that moment that she received more words and above all inner visions
of Jesus. Some years afterwards (in 1562), Teresa began to produce a
written work in which she herself was to be the narrator and source. Here
two actions are inseparable from mystical experience: the foundation of a
new community and the recording of the initial experience in an authorized
writing. These two interdependent actions, which bring about the
transition towards an institution, were both induced by the mystical
experience. A mystic feels called sooner or later to produce a rule of life or a
kind of prayer which crystallizes her or his own experience. The new
community which a mystic desires to assemble will have the mission of
receiving, making visible and transmitting the experiential wisdom
entrusted through the mediation of writing.

John of the Cross is a model by virtue of the status that he gives to
mystical experience in his meditation on the Transfiguration in the *Ascent
of Mount Carmel*.[2] With the New Law, the fullness of revelation given in
Jesus deprives us of any reason for making requests of God in order to
obtain from him a specific response through a vision or a particular
message.

In giving us, as he did, his Son, which is his Word – and he has no other – God spoke to us all together, once and for all, in this single Word, and he has no occasion to speak further.[3]

The logic of this text would seem to exclude every form of particular contact with God today in favour of pure and simple adherence to faith in the Word of God in Jesus. Anyone who wanted to ask questions of God would be looking for more revelation than was his or her due. But the amazing thing here is that John of the Cross rightly finds support in the fullness of the mystery of Jesus as a basis for mystical experience. In fact God could reply to anyone who asked questions:

If I have spoken all things to you in my Word, which is my Son, and I have no other word, what answer can I make to you or what can I reveal to you which is greater than this? Set your eyes on him alone, for in him I have spoken and revealed to you all things, and in him you will find yet more than you ask and desire . . . I have spoken to you, answered you, declared to you and revealed to you, in giving him to you as your brother, companion and master, ransom and prize.[4]

In a paradoxical way the reply attributed to God is as it were a figure of mystical experience. In fact the sole content of God's response is to make heard once again the word which is the climax of the revelation of the Son in his Transfiguration: 'This is my beloved Son, with whom I am well pleased; listen to him' (Matt. 17.5).[5] The only cognitive content of experience is scripture, with nothing added. However, there is a present experience, since it is God himself who gives to the believer once again this word of scripture in a personal context. Instead of being a text stored away in an archive, scripture again becomes word, that is, an act of God to call men and women to obedience in faith.

Here we have the two components of a mysticism of pure faith. The role of scripture is to authenticate mystical experience, the objective content of which it confirms. As for mystical experience, it unveils the power of salvation which there is in scripture, realizing it in a human life: 'for I am not ashamed of the gospel: it is the power of God to the salvation of whoever believes' (Rom. 1.16).

Scripture, the source of faith, is the criterion for the discernment of mystical experience. Now scripture is presented and interpreted by human beings who are referred to the magisterium of the church. For the same reason, when mystics come to produce texts and found new communities, they seek to obtain authorization from the church authorities for their initiatives. Mystical experience does not lack innovative force, but it usually brings with it a call for recognition by the church. This confirmation institutes, in the received forms of life and thought, what has been the shock of an encounter and the striking of a spark.

This model will help us to understand one of the contemporary forms of the mystical quest: the charismatic renewal.

II. Welcoming the Word as gift

The charismatic renewal is a preparation for what the Holy Spirit can give as mystical grace. Here everything takes place in relation to scripture. The essential element in the spiritual experience of renewal consists in receiving the Word of God as a *gift*. Its forms of expression and organization are contingent and stamped by culture. The source of the social bond in the renewal, which gives it power, is the shared recognition of the Word as God's gift. It is precisely through this that the charismatic experience is open towards the institution. In order to identify better the global nature and dynamic of this process, which runs through the life of the whole church, I shall go on to contrast and compare the relationships between sectarian discourse, critical discourse and charismatic discourse. These three forms of discourse relate to the discourse of the institution in such a way as to challenge it, each in a different way.

These four forms of religious discourse stand in contrast, but in so doing appeal to one another. They can only be seen and understood as elements in a single global process by which the members of the church try to preserve or rediscover a social identity which has been put in question. What makes it difficult for us to experience and interpret this process is that the different people involved in it cannot but be situated in one of these movements, and are not able at the same time, in a kind of balancing act, to engage in the other forms of discourse which are in opposition to their own and yet interconnected with it. These moments are not limited and successive slices of time that one can go through and leave behind in a determined order. They are modes in the relationship of the believer to the language of faith. Where social agents, weighed down by the specific form of their reappropriation of this language, usually feel the discourse of others to be dissonant or antinomian, they can sense the breadth of the process of the word of which they represent only one instance in the quest for truth. We can present this process in a diagram which suggests the articulation of these moments and the dynamism of the word which supports them and opens them to one another:

institutional discourse	sectarian discourse	critical discourse	charismatic discourse	institutional discourse
word ordained distributed	word reified mastered	word expressive privatized	word received immediately	word given which becomes law

(a) Institutional discourse

Here the institution denotes the bishops and those to whom they delegate part of their responsibility for government and teaching. Their discourse relates electively to the confession of faith, a verbal act by which the group of believers presents itself as a plural subject ('We believe'). The recurrent intention of institutional discourse is to maintain an accord in the group of believers, with a concern to actualize the formulations of faith.

Institutional discourse is more than anything an appeal to the unity of the group of believers by giving the subject of what is said a new context in the solidarity of the group; or what is said is primarily a shared identical act. In this perspective, the language expressing a belief is above all the action of the group which gives the language to its members. What raises questions in times of crisis is that the institution holds a position close to the source of the language. In fact institutional discourse seeks to bring out the origin of the word which is the gift of God. This is what sectarian, critical or charismatic discourse contest, each in its own way.

One could see here three forms of mystical challenge to the institution, each of which gives priority to a different aspect of the continued incarnation of the Word of salvation, accentuating different functions of language. What is common to the three challenges is suffering in the face of the all too human opaqueness of the institution which bears the hidden treasure of the Word of life. To use an image which recurs in John of the Cross, the ministers of the church are like the soldiers of Gideon who attack the camp of the Midianite enemy by night (Judg. 7.16–20):

All the soldiers of Gideon carried lamps in their hands and did not see them, since they were hidden in the darkness of the jars which enclosed them. Once these jars were broken, the light appeared.

Do we now have to break the earthen vessels which bear the treasure that is the hidden glory of the Risen Christ (II Cor. 4.7)?[6]

(b) Sectarian discourse

Sectarian discourse overdoes the language of faith at each of the points where it has been challenged. The attraction of sectarian discourse is the profound nostalgia which underlies it: the quest for an absolute language which might escape the precarious and obscure condition of the sign. This discourse idealizes the form of the statement like the code bringing together the usual expressions of belief. It is the dream of a language without metalanguage, a univocal language in which a word denotes just one thing. All at once, words tend to replace things. Instead of being a guardian of the language of faith, the institution becomes its prisoner. Language is presented as the first institution, without any need of subjects to enunciate it. Adherence to the faith tends to give way to allegiance to a knowledge crystallized in an idealized system of signs and rules. To hide the fragilities of language, the code which rules it is absolutized, giving an illusion of mastery while imprisoning it in repetition.

Integralists and fundamentalists, for all their basic differences, are perhaps both engaged in the mystical quest for a language of faith whose purity will open it immediately to the mystery of God without the work of interpretation, and the text of time.[7]

(c) Critical discourse

Critical discourse tends to suspend the content of what is said and its referential function in the face of the deceptions brought about by language, a precarious representative of the absent presence. With the disqualification of the language received, the subject is set up as the first authority. This is the expressive function of the language which comes to be privileged ('what *I* believe . . . '). Critical language first presents the personal poem of the subject. Now the law of language compels us to renounce something of personal experience in order to understand the experience of others in the language in which it is condensed: this is a necessary condition for being heard. The critical trend is the nostalgia of a love song which wants to be above the law of language. In the preferential bond, everything is mediation!

(c) Charismatic discourse

While keeping features in common with sectarian discourse and critical discourse, charismatic discourse differs by discreetly beginning a return towards institutional discourse.

Charismatic discourse takes over from sectarian discourse in the fidelity which it rediscovers in the given, which is the objective content of the language of faith. But here this fidelity does not derive so much from a heritage as from a subjective experience. Charismatic discourse takes over from critical discourse in the central place that it accords to the present life of the believer. The 'charism' consists in the welcoming of the word as gift. The charism is a present gift of God to a believer for the service of the church. It is always of the order of the word, whether this be prayer or teaching, advice or commandments. The charisms which are most open to being heard, like glossolalia or prophecy (a message transmitted in the name of God), should draw attention more to their actual origin (the close intervention of the God of the Word) than to the form in which they are expressed.

Here the act of expression is based on a close and personal relationship to the one to whom the word relates: God, who gives it to be spoken. Caught in the trap of a strangeness which is difficult to analyse, those who have observed the way in which charismatic words have been delivered have been preoccupied with the form of the discourse, whether the sounds of glossolalia or the structure typical of testimonies of conversion. They have wanted to see this manifest content always as deriving from a cultural heritage, leaving essential mechanisms aside. The decisive element of charismatic discourse is not the particular form of what is being said but the allegiance it arouses among everyone while offering itself as a gift. As a cultural fact, charismatic experience is the rediscovery of language starting from the fundamental condition of learning it, which is receptivity or hearing. Those who take part in the experience are caught up in the illusion of escaping language. Charismatic discourse remains a human language through the different forms of the spoken acts. Those who receive the Word of God leave their stamp on it in the very act of receiving it.

Charismatic experience relates to the present origin of the word, which is the lordship of the risen Christ, communicated in the fire of the Spirit. 'If with your lips you confess that Jesus is Lord and if in your heart you believe that God has raised him from the dead, you will be saved' (Rom 10.9). Every mystical experience involves hearing a word of scripture again and expressing it historically. The life of Ignatius of Loyola was modelled on a few verses from the hymn in Philippians: 'He humbled himself, becoming obedient to death, even death on a cross. Therefore God highly exalted him and bestowed on him the name which is above every name' (Phil. 2.8–9). The whole obedience of Jesus to the Father entitled him to receive sovereign authority over all ransomed humanity. The centre of Ignatian contemplation is the movement of the filial obedience of Jesus in his humanity.

As for St John of the Cross, if the whole of his life is inspired by a passion for the beauty of the face of the risen Christ, the centre of his contemplation is also the humility of Jesus, but explicitly taking into account the secret of the Incarnate Word. Hidden in the bosom of the Father, the Son of God expresses his essential poverty in the hidden life of Nazareth. Here the humility of Jesus is represented by the detachment and reception which are open to the fullness of the being of the Father. From this stems the call to the wilderness, to put him in the presence of the absoluteness of God.

These two examples lead me to suggest a possible model for the mutual enriching of contemporary mystical experiences and the life of the church. It is enough to remember two features of the spiritual way rediscovered in the charismatic renewal. In the mystery of the lordship of Christ, what is emphasized is the close presence of the Shepherd who knows each of his sheep and calls them by name (John 10.3). Furthermore, the call for recognition by the institutional church is encouraged by the conviction that everything that makes up our lives is given by God, beginning from the word which is the light of our path. The desire to live out everything under the sign of abandonment to God who provides for us leads to a new emphasis on the practice of obedience. Some emphases can be heard: the recourse to scripture, the song of hope, the call to community life, the service of the poor, witness to the Easter faith. These flickers of flame in every race and every tongue will only last and spread if it proves possible to localize the active source of the fire which is none other than the very life of the church as a continuation of the Spirit of Pentecost. So if there is to be an opportunity for renewal in the church by a mystical experience, this experience must be translated, looked for and made accessible by a deep and broad understanding which goes beyond the cultural process. Only recourse to the recognized masters of the experience of the Spirit of God will provide the tools to decipher the ways and the demands of a true encounter with the God of Jesus Christ, who is also the condition for deepening it and making it endure – in other words the source of its renewal. What the church can contribute, bringing from its treasure things new and old, is the knowledge of the great mystics who disclose the spiritual pedagogy contained in Holy Scripture, making it intelligible and creating an opportunity for its communication to every contemporary mystical experience.

III. The path of the sources

In the second redaction of his Spiritual Canticle, John of the Cross depicts the renewal of spiritual life by the blowing of the south wind:

> Stay thee, dead north wind.
> Come, south wind, that awakenest love;
> breathe through my garden
> and make its odours flow.
>   And the Beloved shall pasture among the flowers.[8]

In contrast to the north wind, which by its coldness causes dryness or death, with all that it brings the south wind announces the renewal of spring. The experience suggested is not the initial welcome of baptismal life but a renewal of this life which is a new passage of the Spirit:

> The south wind . . . is a peaceful breeze which causes rain and makes grass and plant grow and flowers to open and scatter their fragrance . . . By this breeze the soul denotes the Holy Spirit, who, as she says, awakens love; for, when this divine breeze assails the soul it kindles it wholly and refreshes and revives it and awakens the will and upraises the desires which had aforetime fallen and were asleep.[9]

With a wealth of imagery from flowering vegetation John of the Cross draws our attention to the priority repeated in his work: the Holy Spirit renews the capacity to love by giving back the love of God. The mystical quest is none other than believing that love exists and that it can inspire, simplify and consume a life. Mysticism reveals the mystery of the church which is the communion of saints, translating into a thousand faces the passionate love of the bride for her absent and hidden bridegroom. But love cannot be content with a song: it calls for the construction of a dwelling in order to share everyday life, so that others can receive there the conditions for living together and learning to love. Perhaps St Vincent de Paul never knew 'signal favours' in his life of prayer. He lived by mystical experience the pure and essential reality which is love of neighbour, made effective by a political understanding. The contribution of mysticism to the church is the arousal of generosity in life in a heroic gift of the self. Half-measures result in a moroseness which is the most insidious trial in the quest of God, the recurrent pattern of *accidie* in a society which has no project to bring it together and no goal to mobilize it. The whole point of mystical experience is to restore their infinite value and taste of eternity to simple words and everyday actions. This is no more and no less than the effectiveness of love which can take all the banality of repetition from repeated words and open the everyday circle to the presence of the hidden Kingdom. Mysticism must not be unrealism in the face of human needs, but the intuition of the beginning of the building of the city of God in our obscure and limited enterprises. The prophet is not one whose task is to contradict, but one who divines the reasons for hope: 'he held firm, seeing the invisible' (Heb. 11.27). The more mystical experience deepens and integrates the totality of human life, issuing in a spiritual sense of the hidden presence of God, a fleeting intuition in the service of love, the more it issues in solidarity with all human beings and praise of the beauty of creation. To go to the source of everything, mysticism culminates when like the life of all the baptized it is received through the rediscovery of divine filiation learned in the church. Its role is to reveal the mystery of the calling of each individual. It can release from the depth of each individual the desire that is most censured by our dominant culture, namely the desire for God.

It remains for me to bring out two conditions for the viability of the mystical quest. The first will be the patience advised by John of the Cross. The second will be the reappropriation of scripture along the lines of Ignatius of Loyala. In the last part of the Spiritual Canticle, having given a glimpse of a stable state of peace in the union of the love of God resonating with the universal harmony of the world, John of the Cross plunges into the heart of reality which is the Wisdom of the Crucified Word:

> There are great depths to be fathomed in Christ. For he is like an abundant mine with many recesses containing treasures, of which, for all that men try to fathom then, the end and bottom is never reached. Rather, in each recess men continue to find new veins of new riches everywhere, as St Paul said of Christ himself in these words: in Christ dwell hidden all treasures and wisdom (Col. 2.3), whereinto the soul cannot enter and whereto it cannot attain unless first, as we have said, it pass through the strait place of exterior and interior suffering into the divine wisdom . . . It cannot be reached save through great suffering and until the soul has received from God many favours, both in the intellect and in the senses.[10]

Knowledge of the mystery of Jesus calls for a lasting preparation which will be none other than recapitulating long years of the hidden life of Jesus of Nazareth. This part of Christian life would present a vertiginous and impossible demand were it not illuminated and opened up by numerous experiences which come to comfort and enliven each person's understanding and heart. The only authorized mystical knowledge is that which dares to insist on the beginnings and the basic conditions of the life of faith. Spiritual deepening can be recognized in the call to go back to the beginning often, as Teresa of Avila remarks in connection with meditative prayer, centred on attention to Jesus the Saviour and sole Mediator.[11]

In this perspective we can understand the renewed current interest in the pedagogy of the Ignatian exercises among those who seek to deepen their life of prayer.

In the Exercises, which lay down and give form to the conditions for gospel conversion, following his own experience, Ignatius drew on the conviction that had come to him in reading the life of Christ: scripture itself can present a call. The stories of callings continue to speak to us. The images of scripture give us models of the conduct of God in our lives; they illuminate, structure and orientate the life of prayer; today they are still meeting-places between God and ourselves.

This pedagogy inherent in scripture relates to the working of the Spirit in the people of God, in his great witnesses, and in exemplary fashion in Jesus of Nazareth. Scripture today teaches us to follow the way of Jesus, which is the way towards the springs of living water.

If scripture is to rediscover the Word of life (Phil. 2.16) in us in all its actuality and force, it is indispensable that it should be given back to us by human mediation, which re-establishes the place of the production of the word in interpersonal communication. To reappropriate scripture we need to be guided by the advice of someone who has learned to listen to the word of God and who can guide the way of beginners or of those beginning all over again. The point of the intervention of the guide is to help those who trust in her or him to perceive and to follow the various interventions of the Holy Spirit in their lives. Everything here relates to the reception of Holy Scripture. It is the practice of the pedagogy of scripture which makes it possible to welcome, to situate and to orientate on scripture the path of the disciple who is personally confronted. The receptivity of the disciple seeking in scripture the Book of Life will give a real index of his or her openness to the inner calls of the Spirit. The first quality of the guide is to know how to be led by the Holy Spirit. The typical test of the guide is to allow himself or herself to be led off route by the Holy Spirit when the Spirit opens a new way to those whom it accompanies. Without this humility in the guide, no innovation is possible, and any intervention of the Spirit will be stifled the moment it surprises us. Here we have an image of the attitude to a mystical proposition which is to be desired in the church.

Discernment is neither mastery of theoretical landmarks nor an art of suspicion but fundamentally guidance. The first criterion for the intervention of the Spirit is that it encourages and opens up a way. To discern is to help someone to find his or own way, acquire autonomy, cross the threshold of growth and not be imprisoned in illusions but go forward on the basis of the Word of God. What mysticism can bring to the life of the church is the vigour and the joy of hope. What the church brings to mysticism are resources for hope and the words to make it understandable to all. The church can acquit itself of this task by opening up an understanding of scripture through the witness of the great spiritual figures.

Translated by John Bowden

Notes

1. Teresa of Avila, *Autobiography*, ch. 26.
2. John of the Cross, *Ascent of Mount Carmel*, ed. and trans. E. Allison Peers, London 1953, ch. 22, 161–72.
3. Ibid., 163.
4. Ibid., 164.
5. The text continues with this quotation.
6. *Ascent of Mount Carmel*, ch. 9. The figure which recurs in John of the Cross is the hidden presence of the Word of Light in the depths of the soul (cf. the light of the heart in the poem 'Night', and cf. the deepest centre of the soul attained by the Living Flame).
7. My remarks on sectarian or critical discourse are based on W. R. Bion, *Recherches sur les petits groupes*, Paris 1972, 85–6, and A. Vergote, *Interprétation du langage religieux*, Paris 1974, 188f.
8. Stanza 17, in *The Spiritual Canticle and Poems*, ed. E. Allison Peers, London 1934, 281.
9. Ibid., 282f.
10. Ibid., Stanza 37, p. 386.
11. *Autobiography*, chapter XIII.

The Wisdom of Latin America's Base Communities

Victor Codina

I. A difficult topic

To write about Latin American base communities ('ecclesial base communities') at the present moment is not at all easy.

Base communities are not only very numerous throughout Latin America, but they also have a different origin and history in each country. The base communities of Brazil, Mexico and Chile, with a tradition going back many years, are not the same as the base communities of the English- and French-speaking Caribbean, which have been in existence for only a few years. Nor is the style of communities the same in Brazil and in Peru. Central American countries, which have lived through a situation of war, like El Salvador, Nicaragua and Guatemala, have a deep experience of martyrdom in their base communities.

Moreover, even within the same country there are great differences between rural base communities and the base communities of the poor suburbs of the great cities, or between base communities belonging to modern culture and base communities whose culture is indigenous or African American.

More important still, however, writing about Latin American base communities at the present time of change implies confronting the image and myth of Latin America formed by the First World. In Europe and North America many people imagine that Latin America is a continent in which every bishop is a Romero or a Helder Câmara, and every woman a Rigoberta Menchú, every parish a community of communities, every theology professor is a liberation theologian and that every base community exhibits the characteristics that Leonardo Boff attributes to a church incarnate in the oppressed classes [1] The reality is very different.

Again, there is a lack of accessible literature on the topic. In the base communities, as in any base movement, life takes priority over reflection.[2] Many of the real problems and the everyday crises of the communities pass unnoticed by the investigator.

All these real difficulties mean that this article must be modest and somewhat fragmentary, the antithesis of any sort of dogmatism.

II. The new socio-political context

It is already a truism to talk about the changes on the international scene, how we have moved from having two hegemonic blocs, East and West, to polarization around the capitalist mono-bloc. In Latin America only Cuba remains isolated in its socialist insularity.

This situation has profound political, social and also economic consequences for Latin America. The poor really are becoming daily more numerous and poorer. Even worse, the inhuman rigidity of the neoliberal model being implanted throughout Latin America is now being made worse by the lack of a socio-political or economic alternative.[3]

Latin America in this past decade has also exchanged military governments for democracies, which may be weak and allow little participation and much corruption, but are in the end democracies.

This new situation has significant repercussions on the lives of the ordinary people and even of the base communities. Many of those who looked to the base communities, in the time of the military dictatorships, for a space of freedom are now finding in trade unions and political parties ample scope to take part in union and political activity.

Those who fought against military dictatorships and had some sort of socialist alternative as their programme now find themselves suddenly without an enemy and without a programme. Even the language of only a few years ago (structural change, revolution) has become exhausted and outdated.

Brazil may be the place in which the political dimension of the base communities is strongest, as was shown in the support given by many of their members to the Workers' Party (PT) in the 1989 presidential elections. There was even a theological debate (notably between Frei Betto and Clódovis Boff) about whether it was appropriate for Christians to support political parties as individuals or as members of the base communities.

Ten years ago, in April 1984, during a visit to Nicaragua, I was invited to take part in a retreat for base communities in a Managua Jesuit retreat house. On the second day I was told that my contribution would be postponed because we were to be visited by an official Cuban government delegation which wanted to meet the Nicaraguan base communities.

The three Cubans limited themselves to asking the members of the base communities if they regarded religion as opium, if it was possible to be both a Christian and a revolutionary, if the church was linked to the bourgeoisie, what the Kingdom of God and heaven meant to them, what the gospel meant, and so on.

The Nicaraguans answered with admirable clarity and boldness, giving authentic testimony of their faith. It was like the Latin American version of the Acts of the Apostles.

Ten years have passed. I doubt very much if Cuba today would send anyone to find out about the life of the Latin American base communities.

III. The new church context

This is also a familiar topic. To avoid repeating truisms, I will concentrate on the general conference of Latin American bishops in Santo Domingo in October 1992.[4]

The second Latin American bishops' conference at Medellín in 1968 said that the Christian base communities are 'the primary and principal nucleus of the church which should, at its own level, take responsibility for the richness and expansion of the faith, and for the worship which is its expression. The community is the initial cell of the church structure, and the centre of evangelization, and currently the prime factor in human advancement and development' (Medellín 15,10).

According to the Puebla conference in 1979, base communities are a cause for joy and hope for the church (Puebla 96), their vitality is beginning to produce its fruit (97, 629, 641–42): 'they are an expression of the church's preferential love for the simple people', to whom they give 'the chance to participate in the work of the church and in the commitment to transform the world' (643).

In comparison with this broad view, backed by the teaching of Paul VI (*Evangelii Nuntiandi* 58), Santo Domingo, perhaps more in the line of *Christifideles Laici* (26) and *Redemptoris Missio* (51) consistently brings the base communities back into the parish ('a living cell of the parish', 61, 'seeking to integrate them into the parish', 63). It also seems to reduce them to mere communities 'of faith, worship and love' (61), equivalent in practice to other lay movements. It was no accident that in the first drafts of the Santo Domingo document, the base communities were placed on the same level as the lay movements, until these were moved to the chapter on the laity (102).

We thus seem to be in a process of pastoral readjustment (C. Boff), recentring (J. Comblin), parochialization, in which the base communities, despite expressions reaffirming their validity (SD 63), no longer seem to embody the hope of the church, to be its basic cell, but at most a parish missionary or solidarity group (SD 63).

As Marins says, 'In its references to base communities, the Santo Domingo document – at least in its final version – is the thinnest bishops' document so far at the level of general conferences of bishops.'[5]

Like the ants that bite the growing point of wheat grains to prevent them from sprouting and allow them to be stored for food instead, the new situation in the church seems to have stifled the originality of the base communities, turning them into one more item on a list of parish groups. The base communities have never refused to participate in the communion of the church (at parochial, diocesan and universal level), but now they are being turned into just another parish group. Many observers feel that a fundamental decision has been made to back the so-called lay movements instead of the base communities. Santo Domingo was one more symptom of this.

What can be the reasons for this anxiety in some circles of the church about base communities? It must be the fear that, in both politics and church affairs, the base communities will escape from hierarchical control and from the traditional parochial model, because, while maintaining a spirit of full communion, they have become aware of their autonomy as lay people in the church.

Fortunately, many members of base communities are not aware of these ecclesiastical complications and live their church life quite naturally and normally, drawing support from those pastors and sectors of the church that encourage them and have made their priority option for them. This is sufficient to enable them to live their ecclesial communion with the local and universal church.

IV. The challenge of the charismatic groups and new religious movements

While many of those who were active in base communities in the years of dictatorship have left them for open activity in parties or trade unions, others have abandoned the base communities and joined movements of Catholic charismatic renewal or even choose to join the so-called new religious movements. Some groups in the church have attributed this exodus to the excessive politicization of the base communities.

It is certainly true that the human race today shows a thirst for the sacred and the religious, even though often this may be ambiguous and even clearly alienating. Whatever the cause, however, it is undeniable that especially Pentecostal movements, whether Catholic or Protestant, have a great attraction for the public.

It has been frequently observed, for example by Carlos Mesters, that the poorest of the poor today are not members of base communities but of Pentecostal churches and sects. José Comblin too believes that Pentecostalism today is a great sign of the times, as the Reformation was in the sixteenth century, except that the Reformation started in alliance with the bourgeoisie and the Pentecostal movement is linked to lower social strata, to the culture of the excluded.[6]

This situation poses a series of questions for the base communities, especially as regards their relationship to the poorest of the poor and their religion. At the same time, however, it opens up possibilities for a new grass-roots ecumenism.

V. The present situation: are the base communities in crisis?

It will be no surprise to anyone that this new context, running through socio-economic issues, politics, culture, the church and religion, should be affecting the base communities.

Many people talk about a crisis of the base communities, though this is a crisis of quality rather than quantity, because base communities are continuing to increase in some countries, but their identity seems to be in question and unclear. Certainly, many of those who talk about the crisis of the base communities and the crisis of liberation theology are partisan, and are layering on the paint in an effort to show that this is all something belonging to the past.

On the other hand, the communities themselves are often aware of the situation of crisis through which they are passing.

A joke, which has a basis in fact, will illustrate the point. In 1990 some young German theology students went to Oruro in the Bolivian *altiplano* to meet and study the base community movement, which had been extremely vigorous in the 1980s. In Oruro they were told that the base communities were in a process of restructuring and they were advised to go to Brazil, where the base communities had a stronger tradition. Once in Brazil, they heard from the Brazilians about the crisis the base communities were undergoing as a result of the political change brought about by the advent of democracy, and they were advised to head for Peru and study the base communities in the shanty towns of Lima. When they got to Lima the Peruvians told them that because of the Shining Path guerrilla movement the base communities were going through a difficult time, and they suggested they visited the base communities in Oruro . . .

The question remains open: is there really a crisis and what sort of crisis?

VI. An emerging new style: a new ecclesiogenesis

The base communities were not invented in a labaoratory or in a seminar on pastoral method, but in life, and life is always new and creative. It is true that there is a base-community style that may be in crisis, but life goes on and the people, with their common sense and wisdom, are able to adapt to new social and church situations.

We are witnessing a new style of base communities, in which, without a break with an earlier tradition, new paths are opening up and new aspects being emphasized.

I am aware that it is dangerous to over-schematize, but in order to clarify and systematize what is happening I shall venture to present dialectically some of the changes we are going through.

From the political to the social and civil. It is not that the political dimension in the broad sense has disappeared from the consciousness of the base communities, but because political parties have suffered a loss of credibility people prefer to act in the social domain (solidarity) and in civil society: groups and associations of neighbours, young people, women, for human rights, in defence of land rights, in defence of life, etc.

From the Exodus to the Exile, from changing structures to survival and defence of everyday living standards in a period of neoliberalism. People no longer see much chance of a rapid change of structures, still less of the Left coming to power; they prefer to fight for survival, to defend ordinary life in the daily situation of the people. This is very different from the privacy championed by postmodernism: there is resistance, there is a fight for life, but without the perhaps slightly naive optimism of the 1970s, when people thought that liberation was round the corner. There is less sense of affinity with the Exodus, and more with the Exile, a time of patience and resistance, waiting for better days.

From prophecy and apocalyptic to the Wisdom tradition. Prophecy has not been abandoned,[7] nor is it seen as unnecessary, nor has it been replaced by an alienating mysticism. Nor have the idols of death or the beasts of the apocalypse disappeared. What is happening is that Christian experience is now more connected to the wisdom of the people in everyday life, with a more practical, down-to-earth knowledge, without the mystical enthusiasm of revolution, with the realism of everyday life and its poverty, its prose, its vulgarity, its contradictions, in a constant desire to win, to fight for one's own life and those of others, in a spirit of faith and hope in God. The prophetic element, while not disappearing, seems to be giving way to the Wisdom tradition, the wisdom of Proverbs, the delicate sceptical irony of Qoheleth/Ecclesiastes, to the patience of Job, who agonizes about God's silence in the face of evil, to confident prayer with the psalms, but also the love feast of the Song of Songs.

From church élitism to popular religion. The base communities do not look down on the rest of the people, as may have been the case at one time, but feel part of the people along with everyone else, including the various expressions of popular religion, in which they take part and which they try to deepen with the Word. It is part of the Wisdom approach to be able to recognize all the wealth of all human traditions, including cultures and religions, without any sort of fundamentalism or dogmatism.

From simple social analysis to acknowledging the role of culture. The base communities are abandoning the rather rigid see-judge-act model in which the 'see' was predominantly socio-economic, and are enriching it with other elements such as cultural mediation, celebration, respect for the characteristics of each group, recognition of difference. There is no abandonment of socio-economic analysis of the neo-liberal social model whose effects they feel in their own flesh, but it is supplemented with other anthropological and cultural elements, since the people too do not live by bread alone, but need celebrations to nourish their hope and anticipate utopia.

From voluntarism in action to the experience of gratuitousness. If at certain times the base communities were marked by a political commitment biased towards activism and moralism, now they situate their social and civil commitment in a broader context, in a climate of prayer, of thanksgiving for everyday life, for the experience of community, in an atmosphere of faith and prayer that may sometimes resemble that of some charismatic communities.

From a patriarchal church to a family community with a feminine face. The role of lay ministry is nothing new in the base communities, nor is the fact that many base communities are composed of and led by women, but what is new is the growing awareness of the role of women in society and church, and that the church should offer ample space for women to participate and reflect the maternal face of God. The more Wisdom-oriented and down-to-earth dimension I talked about before is undoubtedly connected with this presence of women in the base communities.

These features of the ecclesiogenesis that is emerging in many places, of course with different emphases in each place and historical context, are relatively new as compared with the traditional characteristics of the base communities of the 1970s and 1980s.

VII. Assessment and challenges

There is no doubt that these characteristics can be given a spiritualist and reductionist interpretation, as though the base communities were gradually turning into ordinary parish prayer or liturgy groups, without any special commitment, with no impact on society or church, without prophecy. It could be claimed that they had merged with Pentecostal or charismatic renewal groups. That might be what some groups in the church would like.

But the interpretation I suggest is different.

The base communities, with the wisdom characteristic of the people, and specifically of women, have realized that what is important now is not to repeat models or slogans of the past that do not meet the needs of the present, but to live the new *kairos* in today's new socio-economic and church context.

Rather than attempting a direct battle against the present economic and church system, which would be fruitless and in the end frustrating, the base communities have chosen to live a new and different style of society and church. It is a communal and organized model, in solidarity with the most deprived, human, respectful of differences, accessible to the poorest. It is concerned with the community's everyday problems: jobs, transport, food, illness, housing, schools, drunkenness, moral disorders, abandoned children, single mothers, old people, with a faith united to life, integrated with cultures, celebrated in fiestas, a faith which nourishes the people's hope. Rather than confronting the current church and parish system, they offer alternatives of a new model of church, a lay, participatory church, in which all are ministers and missionaries, with a plurality of services, in which the poor, and among them women and young people, are beginning to be the planners and leaders of evangelization.

Some people will certainly see this new style as an abandonment of the primitive ideal of the base communities. In fact it is a step forward, not a step back. This slow work of piecing together a new social and church fabric, starting from the community, freely and with the participation of all, is at root a prophetic leaven with huge consequences for today's neoliberal society, dominated by consumerism, discrimination and individualism, and also for the church of today, with its nostalgias for a Christendom, whether old style or new style.

It is not a cowardly flight or even a tactical retreat; it is a reinforcement of the community and its hope, replenishing faith with the Word, a moment of gestation, in the hope that one day all this will bear its fruit. The woman of Revelation (Rev. 12) does not engage the Dragon directly; her strategy is to live life amid the pangs of childbirth and then to withdraw to the wilderness for a time. The base communities today are acting like the woman who mixes a little yeast with three measures of flour and waits for the mixture to rise (Matt. 13.33).

Latin America's base communities, even though not all of them are conscious of this or can put it into words, are assisting at the birth of an alternative model of society and church, creating alternative visions to the neoliberalism of today and to the revolutionary ideas of the 1970s, visions that can energize society and church.

Of course, all this is also a great challenge for the base communities and implies great discernment if they are not to be diverted from their truth path.

As darkness gathers in the neoliberal world and in the church, the base communities go forward with the Lord, like the disciples on the road to Emmaus, learning to share life, Word and Bread. The Spirit of the Lord, which raised them up, continually guides them, even now, with her wisdom.

Translated by Francis McDonagh

Notes

1. Boff, *Ecclesiogenesis. The Base Communities reinvent the Church*, New York and London, 1986, 10–22.

2. Nonetheless here are some sources: José Marins and his team, 'Las Cebs son termómetro de la Iglesia', *Pastoral Popular* 229 (Santiago de Chile, June 1993), 9–13; Berma Klein Goldewijk, 'Basic Church Structures: Consolidation or Crisis? New Church Structures without Official Recognition', *Concilium* 1992/5, 98–105; P. Richard, 'La Iglesia de los pobres en la década de los 90', *Pasos* 28 (San José de Costa Rica, 1990), 10–16; P. Richard, 'La fuerza histórica de los pobres', San José de Costa Rica, 1988; Gabriel Ignacio Rodriguez, 'Relação entre as comunidades eclesiais de base e a hierarquia', *Perspectiva teológica* 21, 1989, 51–70; J. Comblin, 'La Iglesia latinoamericana desde Puebla a Santo Domingo', in J. Comblin, J. I. González Faus, J. Sobrino (ed.), *Cambio social y pensamiento cristiano en América Latina*, Madrid

1993, 29–56; R. Muñoz, 'Experiencia popular de Dios y de la Iglesia', *Cambio social y pensamiento cristiano*, 161–79; Various, *Santo Domingo. Ensaios Teológico-Pastorais*, Petrópolis 1993; Vicariato de Sucumbíos, *Guia de las comunidades para la Iglesia y el mundo*, Lago Agrio, Ecuador, 1990; *CEBs, Una nueva forma de ser Iglesia*, Santa Cruz, Bolivia, 1993.

3. *Neoliberalismo y pobres. El debate continental por la justicia* , Santafé de Bogotá 1993.

4. V. Codina and J. Sobrino, *Santo Domingo '92. Crónica testimonial y análisis contextual*, Santander 1993; 'Santo Domingo en el caminar de la Iglesia', *Páginas* 119 (Feb. 1993); V. Codina, 'Nuevos rostros en Santo Domingo', *Páginas* 122 (Aug. 1993), 49–61; N. Arntz (ed.), *Retten, was zu retten ist? Die Bischofsversammlung in Santo Domingo zwischen prophetischen Freimut und ideologischen Zwang*, Lucerne, 1993; CELAM, *Santo Domingo Conclusions*, Washington and London, 1993; G. Gutiérrez and others, *Santo Domingo and After. The Challenges for the Latin American Church*, London 1993.

5. J. Marins, 'Las CEBs son termómetro de la Iglesia' (n. 2), 12.

6. J. Comblin, 'A nova Evangelização', *Santo Domingo. Ensaios Teológico-Pastorais*, Petrópolis 1993, 215.

7. During the Santo Domingo conference itself, when the bishops were being very reticent about a solemn, public act of contrition for the abuses of the Conquest and the first evangelization, it was the CEBs of Santo Domingo who, in spite of all sorts of difficulties with the church authorities and even the police, organized a huge penitential liturgy on 27 October in Plaza Bartolomé de Las Casas, beside the Dominican priory, where Montesinos delivered his famous prophetic homily in defence of the indigenous peoples.

From Exclusion to Discipleship

Gustavo Gutiérrez

While I do not offer this as a general definition of what we mean by mysticism, it is clear that it has something to do with an experience of God in a key of love, peace and joy. In contrast, 'oppression' refers to a situation of poverty, injustice and exclusion, with its resultant suffering and, in many cases, rejection and rebellion. Are these then incompatible human experiences?

On this abstract conceptual level, perhaps the question requires the answer 'yes'. On the other hand, as a matter of fact those who find themselves in these situations are human beings, with all the personal dimensions this implies; they also belong to peoples with a history, culture and vision of the universe. Only in this real context can we fruitfully explore this subject. In doing so we meet people in whom poverty and dispossession mark their faith in God, and this in its turn leaves a mark on the condition of oppression and discrimination.[1]

There is certainly a close relationship between mysticism and politics, which has been the subject of many studies. Without contemplation, prayer, thanksgiving to God there is no Christian life, any more than there is without commitment, solidarity and love of neighbour. The point I am making now is certainly connected with this relationship, but it is not identical with it. Our question is rather: can we talk of a mystical dimension in the faith life of a person who suffers exclusion and injustice and eventually embarks on a path of liberation from these conditions?

An attempt to answer this question presupposes a move from the realm of the individual to a position within socio-cultural contexts, in a historical perspective and to viewpoints from different geographical points on the planet. Above all, however, it requires us to be sensitive to one of the facts most pregnant with consequences for present-day Christianity: the Christian faith has not just begun to spring up, but has also grown and matured in non-Western peoples who have been poor and oppressed for centuries.

Today in the church certain conflicts of interpretation about the times we live in and the challenges they present to us frequently provoke tensions, difficulties and misunderstandings that prevent us from seeing that something much more important than these differences of opinion – even on issues that are obviously important and even urgent – is taking place among us. In a famous article, a sort of balance-sheet of Vatican II, Karl Rahner said that the Council's main significance was that it marked the beginning of a third stage in the life of the church, a period in which it could begin to be genuinely universal.[2]

The vigorous existence of local churches in places geographically and culturally far removed from Europe, the force of their voices, containing accents of pain and hope, the contribution of their theological reflection and the new challenges this brings represent the most important event for the Christian faith in these last years of the second millennium of its history.[3]

This is the context in which we must discuss the subject of mysticism and oppression. The presence of those who are different from Western culture is now established, of course, but it is not always recognized; it will lead us to re-examine central texts of the Christian revelation which can throw light on the process under way and finally indicate the pattern of spirituality represented by the preferential option for the poor.

I. Assimilation and otherness

The Europeans who came to the American continent in the sixteenth century (and from their point of view 'discovered' it) were spontaneously and absolutely convinced of their human and cultural superiority to the inhabitants of these lands.[4] The peoples whom they began to call 'Indians' had, in their eyes, no rights that could call in question the privileges in which they gloried as discoverers and conquerors. The fate of these peoples was to hand over all they possessed to the newcomers and finally to labour for them.

The majority of missionaries took the same view. As regards the Gospel, the Indians – lacking religious values – were simply *tabula rasa* (Columbus used the phrase in his diary), a blank page on which everything was still to be written. Some even thought this could be done by force and wars, others, to varying degrees, called for more human treatment, but the basic acceptance of the asymmetry between Europeans and the Indian population was the same.

In this perspective, the best fate that could befall the inhabitants of these lands was to be absorbed by the superior culture and religion. This policy of assimilation not only did not prevent prior destruction, it presupposed it and moreover presented itself as a form of destruction. This attitude, assimilationist and colonialist, has not died. The economic and political preponderance of the North Atlantic countries has kept it alive; even more, the power and ubiquitousness of the communications media have made this attitude an everyday reality, and to a great extent one generally accepted.

This mentality is also expressed in the Christian world. It would seem that many people believe there is no other way of being a believer in Jesus Christ than through the Western mental categories and life-style that trace their roots back to a Graeco-Latin past. This is something that the Christian churches to this day have been unable to overcome. The result is a series of misunderstandings and unresolved problems that weigh heavily on the development of the ecclesial communities present in a world that is distant from or alien to that of the North Atlantic.[5]

However, as early as the sixteenth century itself a different attitude from the one we have just described was already present. A handful of missionaries reacted vigorously against the ill-treatment of the Indians, and gradually some of them – notably Bartolomé de Las Casas – began to insist on respect for the culture and customs of the Indian nations. It was not easy for all of them to shake off the conviction of belonging to the highest level of civilization, and it could be said that in a sense they did not succeed in this completely and in all areas. But they journeyed firmly in this direction.

Las Casas believed that if we want to understand what is happening we have to adopt the point of view of the inhabitants of the Indies. 'If we were Indians,' the Dominican bishop said, 'things would take on a different colour for us.' The discovery of otherness – a costly, but clear-sighted process – marks not only his pastoral action and theological method, but also his spirituality as a Christian. His enormous and bold attempt to understand from within, and to make his compatriots understand, the human sacrifices and the cannibalism practised among the Aztecs – which scandalized the Europeans – is an example of how far he was able to go in this attempt.[6]

Recognizing otherness is still an unfinished task. This was one of the earliest intuitions of liberation theology.[7] The perspective of the 'underside of history' is an obligation still in full force. The perception of the otherness of the poor and oppressed (in social, racial, cultural and gender terms) enables us to understand how they can enjoy a keen sense of God, which does not disdain celebration and joy, in the midst of a situation of expropriation and a struggle for justice. By unknown paths the experience of oppression has turned out to be fruitful ground for the mystical dimension of Christian life.

What seems contradictory or, at best, suspect, to a modern mentality becomes real and full of promise in a different socio-cultural context. And let no one think that I am talking about the practice of prayer as a protection against daily sufferings or religious observance as a shock-absorber to deaden the reaction of rejection provoked by exploitation and contempt. Such situations exist, of course, and not just as exceptions, but they do not account for or explain the whole situation. There are many cases in which the mystical and spiritual perspective is, on the contrary, the best antidote to the use of Christianity as a search for a refuge or a justification of the status quo, and one of the main factors in generating and developing human and Christian solidarity.

Moreover, this complex experience provides criteria for discernment with results that seem simple, but are nonetheless unexpected. For example, I can never forget the distinction I heard made by a woman belonging to a Christian base community: a Christian can live joy in a situation of suffering, but not of sadness. Sadness, she explained, turns you in on yourself and can make you bitter. The Easter perspective of this approach to the experience of the poor is clear, but not everyone achieves it.

In other words, the subject of the mystical dimension in the existence of those who suffer oppression directs us to the situation of the Christian communities that have grown up in what until recently was called the Third World. Their experience of faith is not a simple reflection of what happens where Christianity has been rooted for many centuries. Forced to adapt to the climate of a different environment and feed on a sap fed by other soil, faith has produced rich fruits with a taste slightly different from that which many people were used to, but does that mean that these fruits are less authentic and nourishing?

The establishment of 'winter gardens' to reproduce the European climate in other environments – a practice in which some persist – only leads to artificial situations with no future. The demands of what is today called 'inculturation' – something on which the Latin American bishops at their 1992 general conference in Santo Domingo insisted – go beyond adaptation and call for a revision of mental categories. This will not come about without cases of hesitation and misunderstanding, but also not without determination and courage on the part of those who see this change as essential if the Christian faith is to have a vital presence in the world of today.

At a bound

From being second-class members even of the Christian churches, the oppressed are coming to be full disciples of Jesus. From having their experience of God and their theological reflection underestimated, they are now beginning to enrich the universal Christian community, and this is also happening with the mystical dimension of their faith in a world of poverty, which some mistakenly think leaves no room for gratuitousness or at most summons us to the struggle for justice. The process has been and is long and costly, like that which John describes for us in the supremely important and beautiful ninth chapter of his Gospel.

The story in John 9 introduces us to a person who is clearly, for the evangelist, the model of the disciple. A blind beggar (and so doubly poor) recovers his sight through the action of Jesus. In the sharp dialogues to which this fact gives rise, the former blind man repeats how things happened, how Jesus gave him his sight. What John is doing is insisting on the experience which is at the start of the faith of a person taking the road towards discipleship.

Those who had been accustomed to see the man blind and sitting begging doubt his identity. It can't be the same person: how can this reject possibly now be someone able to see and fend for himself? Those who are insignificant should stay that way; that's how the world is, and any change overturns an order in which everything is in its proper place. We are very familiar with this reaction today as well. There now begins a series of dialogues in which, in a move which is extremely significant and unique in his Gospel, John makes Jesus disappear for twenty-eight whole verses. In his place is none other than the man he has cured and who gradually adopts the status of disciple: the evangelist even puts into his mouth an expression he usually keeps for the Lord: 'I am he' (literally, 'I am,' 9.9). His experience leads him to a simple affirmation, to a first step in his journey as a disciple: he received his sight from 'the man called Jesus' (9.11).

However, the doubts of the man's neighbours are nothing to the aggressiveness the incident provoked in the powerful. The Pharisees believe he was never blind, and that they are faced, not with mistaken identity, but with a deliberate lie: this Jesus cannot have done this. The former blind man does not stop at describing what happened: without fear he goes up another rung and tells the élite of his people that the person who did this 'is a prophet' (9.17).

The dialogue – the dispute – begins to take on a theological flavour. Arguing from their abstract principles, the experts in the Law insist that this Jesus is a sinner and cannot have done what the accused – as he increasingly is – claims. The man starts from his experience and grows in his conviction: 'Do you also want to become his disciples?' he asks ironically (9.27). He is now arguing equal to equal with those who claimed a religious and theological superiority, with those who assumed they knew all about God, and refutes them when he maintains – to the surprise and opposition of the great of his world – that if Jesus 'were not from God, he could do nothing' (9.33).

The author of the Gospel now brings Jesus back. With the experience not just of being healed, but also of meeting Jesus, the new disciple realizes what he now can see and confesses without fear, 'Lord, I believe' (9.38). The light of faith has opened his eyes a second time and radically changed his life. From being excluded, insignificant and despised, he has come to be a disciple, to take Christ's place in the story, to confound those who prided themselves on their knowledge.

This maturation of faith ought to overcome the scepticism of those accustomed to a particular social or religious system, enable them to resist the onslaught of the powerful, to stand up to the pride of those who think they have nothing to learn, to talk on an equal footing to those who boast of an alleged superiority. In a sense the poor and oppressed peoples who have made the Christian faith their own are represented by this beggar blind from birth. Many would have preferred to see them always subject to charity, unable to stand up for themselves and to think out in original ways their path as disciples of Jesus. Of all the Lord's disciples – John likes to call them friends – the man blind from birth is the evangelist's favourite, who, like the poor of this world, has no name. His passage through history and his becoming a disciple is bringing them out of anonymity. Their experience of God, the mystical dimension of their lives, does not appear at the end of the road; it grows little by little out of their state of exclusion and oppression.

The Synoptic Gospels, in accounts that are less detailed but no less significant, give us a similar message in the story of the blind man of Jericho. At the exit from the city a sightless beggar (doubly poor, once more) is sitting by the edge of the road. As Jesus comes by, this man sees what others are unable to see, shouts out 'son of David', and asks him for help (Mark 10.47).

The God of Jesus is none other than the God of the forgotten and excluded, of those people want to silence, which in this case was the reaction of the people around the Lord (cf. Mark 10.48). But Jesus has come for these first, and the prospect of the death he will face very soon in Jerusalem does prevent him from having time for the suffering and the hope of this poor man. He asks him to come near, and the blind man does so, according to the text, 'with a bound' (cf. 10.50), perhaps over the heads of those who were demanding that he be silent.

Jesus does not impose his power on him, does not claim to know what he wants, does not overwhelm him with his help; he asks, 'What do you want me to do for you?' (10.51). Listening is an important element of dialogue, and in this case the Lord makes a space for the beggar to take an initiative and assert himself as a person. The poor are not objects of favour; they are subjects of rights and desires. When the man asks Jesus to make him see, Jesus observes that the blind man has taken an active part in this event: 'your faith has made you well' (10.52). At that moment Bartimaeus – this time we know his name – gets up, leaves the side of the road and sets foot on it, following Jesus as a disciple.

The processes recorded are significant and paradigmatic. The call to discipleship is permanent, and includes in a special way the forgotten and oppressed. The Bartimaeuses of this world have stopped being at the side of the road, they have jumped up and come to the Lord, their lifelong friend. Their presence may upset the old followers of Jesus, who spontaneously, and with the best reasons in the world, begin to defend their privileges. They have discovered – and it cost them an effort to do so – *one* way of being a Christian, and no doubt they think it is *the* way to be a Christian for everyone. This sometimes throws up novel demands for proper conduct in life and in Christian thinking which are not confined to the offices of some church authorities; they are also the result of the exegesis and theology done in the North Atlantic world and even extend to ordinary Christians in those latitudes. They frequently react to the eleventh-hour disciples (workers) with the 'envy' the Gospel describes (Matt. 20.1–16, esp. 15). Clearly the gratuitousness of God's love challenges the patterns we have become used to.

A theocentric option

What is fundamental to the theological experience and reflection that has taken place in Latin America in recent decades is summed up in what we call the preferential option for the poor. The idea – and the phrase – has succeeded in piercing layers of initial resistance and hostility until it finally penetrated the universal magisterium of the church. But there is still a long way to go.

The preferential option came into being in the context of a historical event of vast proportions which we know as the entry of the poor on to the stage of history. This phenomenon takes various forms across the planet. This situation has forced before our eyes with stark clarity the ancient and cruel poverty of the great majority of the world's population, which has come on to the stage of society – as Las Casas said of the Indian nations of his time – with their poverty on their backs. But this situation has also brought into play the energies and qualities of this people. It is a phenomenon not without ambivalences, but challenging and in many respects full of promise, as it has enabled the poor and oppressed to begin to feel in control of their own history, like a person at last in the driving seat of their destiny.

These events revived discussion about poverty in the church, and sent it in new directions. So in Latin America, since July 1967, a distinction has been made between three senses of 'poverty': real (or material) poverty, which is an evil; spiritual poverty in the sense of spiritual childhood, surrender of our lives to God's will; and poverty as solidarity with the poor and protest at the situation in which they live. This emphasis implies a particular analysis of poverty and its causes, presupposes also a biblical basis both for the rejection of this inhuman situation and of the way spiritual poverty is understood, and finally clarifies the reasons – which have nothing to do with any sort of idealism – for Christian commitment in this field.

This impulse was welcomed a year later at the Latin American bishops' conference at Medellín (1968) and gave clarity to a commitment which many were beginning to make. Then, between Medellín and the next conference, at Puebla (1979), this distinction gave rise, within the Christian communities, to the expression 'preferential (spiritual poverty), option (solidarity and protest) for the poor (real poverty)'. This option became a guiding thread for the church's pastoral action, and an important standard for a way of being Christian, that is, for what we call a spirituality, the principal, seminal concern of liberation theology.

The truth is that the ultimate reason for preferring the poor and oppressed does not lie in the social analysis we employ, in our human compassion or in the direct contact we may have with the world of poverty. All these are valid motives, important factors in this commitment, but this option has its real roots in the experience of the gratuitousness of God's love, in faith in the God of life who rejects the unjust and early death which is what poverty means. It is a theocentric option, based on the practice of solidarity and the practice of prayer among us. It is a gift and a task.

The preferential option for the poor is much more than a way of showing our concern about poverty and the establishment of justice. Inevitably, at its very heart, it contains a spiritual, mystical element, an experience of gratuitousness that gives it depth and fruitfulness.[8] This is not to deny the social concern expressed in this solidarity, the rejection of injustice and oppression that it implies, but to see that in the last resort it is anchored in our faith in the God of Jesus Christ. It is therefore not surprising that this option has been adorned by the martyr's witness of so many, as it has by the daily generous self-sacrifice of so many more – ignored by the mass media – who by coming close to the poor set foot on the path to holiness.

The answer to the question about the nature of the mystical dimension in the faith-life of an oppressed person involves understanding the meaning of the preferential option for the poor. And this in turn cannot be seen in its full scope until we become aware of the inculturation of the Christian faith in nations that are poor but rich through a cultural and historical journey different and distant from those of the North Atlantic world.

Faith in the risen Christ is nourished by the experience of suffering, death and also of hope among the poor and oppressed, by their way of relating to each other and to nature, by their cultural and religious expressions. Asserting one's own characteristics does not mean refusing to learn, to be enriched by, to open oneself to, other perspectives. It means rather staying alive to be able to receive and grow. Going to the roots ensures creativity, renews the tree. At the heart of a situation that excludes them and strips them of everything, and from which they seek to free themselves, the poor and oppressed believe in the God of life. Rilke was right when he said that God is in the roots.

Translated by Francis McDonagh

Notes

1. In Latin America for many years now we have talked about a 'people that is oppressed and Christian'. In an Asian context Aloysius Pieris refers to the way '*Poverty* and *Religiosity* seem to coalesce', 'Towards an Asian Theology of Liberation', *The Month* 1340 (May 1979), 148–59: 148 (italics in original)).

2. Cf. *Concern for the Church*, New York 1981. From a theological standpoint, Rahner says, there are three main periods in the history of the church: the period from Jesus to Paul, connected to the Jewish world; the time between Paul and Vatican II, linked to the Western world; and the third period, beginning with Vatican II.

3. This is why J. B. Metz uses the term 'polycentric church', replacing the monocentric church, confined to the West. Cf. 'Theology in the Modern Age, and before Its End', *Concilium* 171, Jan. 1984, 13–17.

4. The same thing happened, *mutatis mutandis*, in the contacts with African and Asian countries. I shall refer mainly to Latin America in this article because I know this situation better, but I have no doubt that the attitudes in question are not limited to this continent.

5. We shall see what happens in this regard during the forthcoming (April-May 1994) synod of the Catholic bishops of Africa.

6. G. Gutiérrez, *En busca de los pobres de Jesucristo. El pensamiento teológico de Las Casas*, Lima 1992.

7. Cf. G. Gutiérrez, *A Theology of Liberation*, New York and London, rev. ed. 1988, 106–20; 'Liberation, Theology and Proclamation', *Concilium*, Vol. 6, No 10 (June 1974), 57–77; 'The Poor in the Church', *Concilium* 104, 1977, 11–16.

8. This is what makes us sensitive to the discourses of justice and gratuitousness that the writer of the book of Job uses to talk about God. Cf. the studies by L. Alonso Schökel subsequently collected in his *Job. Comentario teológico y literario*, Madrid 1983; the excellent article by W. Vogele, 'Job a parlé correctement', *Nouvelle Revue Théologique* (Nov-Dec. 1980), 835–52, and G. Gutiérrez, *On Job. God Talk and the Suffering of the Innocent*, New York and London 1987.

The Blind Spot, The Lack in the Body

Gérard Rolland

*'You wanted me to tell you once more about the interval that brings us
together.*
I need that interval to be, to become.
*It is the interval which frees you. It arouses your desire, opens your
countenance.'*
(Jean Mambrino, 'Le palimpseste')

As we come to the end of a century which has been both so frivolous and so
tragic, in which we are beginning to take stock of the slow obliteration of
the absolutes of History, history, even without its capital, seems to have
become unreadable.

The effort required of us in this issue is certainly not to accept this
verdict. Thus each contributor is bringing to it what he has investigated,
meditated on and put into action, and this work of attention and
discernment leads both to a certain detachment and to quite a decisive
involvement. For my part, in the end I feel led to attempt to give shape to a
body of writing which offers the possibility of space for some premoni-
tions. This is my particular way of keeping clear of the dreary synthesis to
which moralizing thought risks leading us.

In fact I have the impression of having been led by the very thing that I
see coming to birth and appearing in the particular sphere of mystical
experiences to which I am referring here: from the twelfth century, in the
West. It is the birth and as it were the anticipation of a (foolish?) migration
outside the institution, through original, adventurous and sometimes
violent re-enrolments, in an individual body of word and writing, in part
hidden and lacking an incomplete institutional body.

Furthermore, brought within earshot of these 'strange strangers', what
we hear is the dull rumour of today's world. For what among the mystics
has moved and shaken their personal, social and ecclesial body is the very
wave which since then has not ceased to spread in the body of humanity

and is now the experience of the majority. It is this individualization of the relationship of the transcendent which, by its very existence and possibility, is a way of saying to the body of the church, 'You are not everything'. Much more radically and seriously than reports, even difficult ones, relating to the legitimate part of internal control, what the institution feels an intolerable irritation about is this idea which attacks its claim to totality, to being the visible form of the One.

It is usually said that the status of mystics in the church is that they do not have one. But it is perhaps not enough to use the term status to denote the distance of the mystics from the functioning of institutions based on dogmatic integralities. The distance attested by this kind of mystical experience in fact signifies that a church creed is not the revelatory mirror of the whole of our identity.

At the end of the sixteenth century and in the first part of the seventeenth the word mysticism became involved in the attempt to form a 'science of experience'. We may see this as in part an institutional normalization and a kind of neutralizaton of this kind of experience. It should not surprise us that this period is also that of the Tridentine Counter-Reformation from which in part the failure of dialogue with modernity derives. One could even interpret this development as a rescue: mysticism is part of the mystical body by virtue of an eschatological dimension and an eschatological witness. Thus the existence of contemplative institutions provides a place for those on a mystical journey for whom a context could not be found elsewhere.

However, that does not take account of the significant originality represented by the mystical experience which arose at the beginning of our second millennium, at a time when we can recognize a large number of bases and movements which were slowly to construct what we call 'modernity' and which today form our world, a world which, in its autonomy and its increasingly radical distance from religious institutions, is the authentic place where the mystical experience of the hidden God echoes and is prolonged: the space of the 'lack in the body'.

A long time ago Henri de Lubac[1] demonstrated the historical evolution of the patristic scheme of the threefold body of Christ and showed how in the ninth century progressive dissociations were introduced, so that in the thirteenth century the church came to call itself the 'mystical body' without any further link with the eucharist. The imaginary totality conveyed by this term indicates a wound, and thus a lack. In fact the separation between spiritual and temporal had already begun to resound in post-Carolingian society. The monarchical ideology was emancipating itself from its essentially liturgical garb to occupy an autonomous space and to provide the visible cohesion for the social body in its threefold register of values: religious, military and economic. The Concordat of Worms (1122), which was thought to have put an end to the 'Investiture' dispute, expresses sufficiently the inevitable unlinking which took place. This emergence of the legitimacy of a profane sector merely confirms the essential role of the technical and economic development which begins around the year 1000 and increases in quality and quantity in the twelfth century. It has been shown[2] how the boom of the cities and of trade, and above all the development of a theology of work with specializations into trades and the social mobility which this brought about, sparked off and set in train an irreversible process of personalization around the individual conscience.

Certainly, in this world which was demonstrating its secular character the mystical ideal was difficult to rediscover, and the flight from the world and compromises with the age were still expressed in a traditional way. Be this as it may, the 'Charter of Charity' (1118) which fixed the Cistercian rule does not just display spiritual rejection and a rejection of the world: in it, work is promoted as an economic value of such a kind that, some years afterwards, the Cistercian monasteries took part in the take-off of the market economy to such a degree that it has proved possible to claim that they were the ancestors of a kind of capitalism.[3]

When a century later Francis of Assisi said 'our cloister is the world', the world was perceived and received in its positive autonomy and the institution was reduced to fulfilling its totalitarian desire through the metaphor (or more precisely the allegory) of a so-called mystical body. When in the autumn of 1209 or the spring of 1210 Francis went to Rome, where he was received by Innocent III, the latter expressed serious reservations about the movement. However, the next night the pope had a dream: he saw the cathedral of St John Lateran tottering on its foundations and near to collapse. A small, puny man came up, leaned against it and set the building straight. 'Then at the next audience, he gave his oral approval to the rule.'[4]

I have the feeling that this 'oral' is pregnant with meaning. At the moment when the established body sees that it is crumbling and a reality which is not recognized in this body gives meaning to this ec-stasis, the recognition of this 'strangeness' is not inscribed in the institutional order of the written code but is kept at a distance in the oral sphere. Here in a more exact way we can find the distance mentioned above. The testimony of mystical experiences is not a pretension outside or against the institution. It is a break in the self-sufficient institutional body: not only is this not divine nor its own origin, but in addition it does not exist for itself; it exists solely on behalf of that which it is not. The 'mystical way' seeks to say to the apostolic body of the cenacle that it is mortal, perishable, and that the power of resurrection comes to it from Another; to open it to a definitive non-localization which has nothing to do with a reconstruction. To make the point again: it is a way of saying 'You are not all the body'. Talk of the lack in the body denotes the blind spot.

Perhaps here we have to do with the most decisive feature of Christianity as a religion of incarnation: the question of *mediation*. The type of mystical experience to which reference is made here is a way of moving from an understanding of mediation as a unique intermediary, obligated and accredited between two worlds, the secret key of whose homogeneity it possesses. The mystics say that the reality of mediation escapes this ideal and conceptual globalization and has its place – corporally and thus socially, then ecclesially – in a third order which is no longer the unmediated articulation between the heavenly and the earthly, and which exists in the mode of the 'figure' in its own irreducible positivity. In other words, they have only the existential space of their individual body which is in need of socialization, where something happens that breaks the circle which provides security. Thus we can understand the event which is in a way at the heart of the experience of Teresa of Avila as she relates it in her 'Account of the 18 November 1572': that host broken in two which John of the Cross gives her: 'I thought that this Father acted like this, not because he did not have enough hosts but because he wanted to mortify me, because I had told him that I very much liked receiving large hosts.'[5]

This event, in one sense derisory, is important not only for Teresa herself[6] but also for us, in that her narrative expresses a break and a lack. This happens where ecstatic language opens up and takes shape, this bold wandering outside established meaning, by a real subversion of ecclesiastical theological 'culture'.

> '*They told you*
> *you had gone mad because of the One you love.*
> *I told you:*
> *the savour of life is only for the mad.*'
>
>   (Ibn'Arabi)

Apart from showing in its own way that the gospel is not a culture (something which is too often ignored), mystical experience sets in motion the movement of any language which is not to close in on itself. It evades an instituted grammar by taking form and meaning in unforeseen, literally abnormal experiences. What by contrast is normal is for the institution to be irritated by this and to take on a 'controlling' role; this is legitimate, because intentions and usages must be effectively distinguished. It would be ruinous for all language to confuse an objective enunciation with a subjective expression. As I shall go on to say, this is something that happens a great deal today: it calls itself piety and has nothing to do with mysticism.

It is understandable that before attesting, by being put out of it, a lack in the mediation of the institutional body, the mystics resorted to the vocabulary of immediacy. However, I sense that we must not interpret their vocabulary as a new direct line with the transcendent, in such a way that there is an immediacy which is totally detached from any institutional body or which passes over any real incarnation. Certainly it is easy to go wrong if one does not pay attention to the rhetoric, noting that no language is made up only of words but is also affected by the movement which they contain. For example a precise lexicological study of a story by Teresa of Avila – which would need a deep knowledge of Spanish usage in her time and particularly of popular speech – would show how she herself takes care to specify the aim of her vocabulary by so frequently using expressions like: 'I call here . . . what I call . . . ' In short, we are quite simply (what a euphemism!) faced with the difficulties which confront anyone who develops a new intentionality with this indispensable tool, albeit one of which we are not the authors, since language precedes us.

We need to go even further to interpret the language of desire and immediacy. Now we come more to what Louis Massignon would call a rhetorical 'distortion', to the openness of an aesthetic space for a poetic habitability of language. Hence the break with a strictly ontological hermeneutic. Poems and stories, even when doctors and confessors call for explanations of them, remain the evocative source: sermons, impertinent sentences or inflamed letters; anti-social procedures or behaviour, all this indicates a 'potential space',[7] a logical prerequisite to all established order. When the erotic appears in the vocabulary and grammar of the conceptual we have a 'game'. The existential impossibility of inhabiting onto-theological discourse is subverted not by an intention of fusional sublima-tion, but with the aim of play. This is in fact what Stanislas Breton, a logical philosopher who has paid so much attention to the meaning of the 'mystical', calls 'the theorem of limitation'.[8] 'The indicator of the language object moves in the sphere of determination, in the empire of forms. Is it mere coincidence that the people which was so fond of forms also felt – it does not matter much by which way – that every form in the world and in language is based on an "amorph", a pure indeterminate which cannot be reduced either to a horizon of implicit determinations or to the fullness of determinations?' (167). This abstract designation of what is at issue in the mystical use of language is perhaps for all that expressed by a remark of the painter Pierre Soulages: 'As long ago as I can remember, as a child, one day when I was dipping a brush in the ink and making large shapes on paper, someone asked me what I was painting. And I replied, with the paper slashed with black: a snow scene.'

In the same direction, I have the impression that mystical language has some link, in its own way, with the irreplaceable literary genre of midrash to which Emmanuel Levinas attributes 'the power to force the secret of transcendence',[9] because it bears witness to an audacity in looking for meaning beyond dogmatic or even only allegorical interpretations.

Finally, how can one fail to read in this new writing of an immemorial language, a major displacement which I would succinctly denote by the formula 'from the ONE to the OTHER'? For even if the linguistic borrowings from the tradition of Philo or Dionysius the Areopagite continue (and up to Bérulle the latter remains a strong point of reference, since it is a matter of legitimating the 'ecclesiastical hierarchy' in the celestial and liturgical hierarchy *against* the realities of history which separate the visible and the invisible), we have departed from, have almost been driven out of, the original nostalgia of the plenitude of the One. We will no longer be ourselves in a Gnostic operation of return to the matrix. The *a priori* of individual unity replaces and annuls the vision of an antecedent unity; the body is not a minor emanation of the Divine, distant and diffracted, but as body the place where a symbolic work can or must take shape, the un-known in which is brought out only by and in the interplay of the desire of the other. This is achieved only by departing from any institutional body which claims to be in possession of the enunciation and the figuration of the One and the All. It seems to me better in this connection to quote the famous but topical phrase of Michel de Certeau: 'The one who gets detached from the institution becomes a *mystic*'.[10]

The language of immediacy does not denote access to the divine. Besides, where relations with God are concerned, where the official language speaks of presence, of light, of being, mystical language speaks of absence, of night, of nothingness. It envisages a different place of mediation from the institution. It envisages immediacy or at least the truth of a presence in itself. For it is at the heart of the 'subject' that the mediation comes about and it is at this place that it has to be present: at the cost of a desocialization which consists in no longer trusting in the social identities which we bear and to which we are reduced. To the degree that it has not become embodied and taken on meaning in a personal conscience, the word of baptism remains declarative and does not create any significant belonging which can be lived out. Mystical experience does not at all deny that the sacramental regime is realized in a body which is historically visible, in which 'what is said is what is done'; it says that the truth of its realization is not of the order of the *ex opere operato* but belongs to the symbolic order that requires as a place of mediation the individual conscience which animates a body that is personal and always singular. It speaks of a universal which has a meaning only in the particular.

> *'The darkness opens up to the brightness.*
> *Every presence turns*
> *into another,*
> *so many presences which are open*
> *one to the other.*
> *And in the brightness the darkness opens up.'*
> (Jean Mambrino, 'L'oiseau coeur')

I expect that the reader will already have detected that the few feelings which take shape in this way of writing history are of an other age and yet that they can give our present something to read.

Within the general plan for this issue the working title suggested to me was: 'The Desire for the Immediacy of God and Institutional Control'. It has become apparent to me that the problem implied by the subject was more difficult to raise than to resolve. You will remember the game which consists of joining together certain numbered points in such a way as to produce a silhouette: that is in fact what is being proposed here. The figure which appears in this way does not lead us to consider the contemporary religious scenarios as mystical. Using the uncertain and enigmatic incantation of André Malraux ('the twenty-first century will be religious [others say mystical] or it will not be'), what emerges from the sphere of piety is taken to be a significant and strictly mystical dimension. This is a grave distortion and a no less grave confusion between piety and faith. Mysticism is of the former order and not the latter. It cannot accommodate the projectors, decibels and enthusiasms of media shows. It is an outmoded institutional attempt to reincorporate, under the form of catering to religious need, an exiled reality which definitely cannot be recovered. Here is certainly not the soaring music or the alleluias which accompany the concern for a new look which Vatican II in part dared to give the world. Perhaps with naivety, and doubtless in too simply declarative a way, this council in faith took note of the role of mystical reality in modern experience. The communiocratic behaviour which is evident today does not take this line. It is also fraudulent to claim that the reusing of later and more topical forms of piety (those of the last two centuries) corresponds to the 'popular religion' of the smallest and the simplest. That is where the blind spot is; to think that the mystical dimension is reserved for some of us and piety is for most people. No, today the majority of people are experiencing a marginalization of the church, the nature and significance of which are mystical. The world is full of itinerants who are not seeking to make another church and who do not think themselves the repositories of a secret truth; they are uneasy prowlers, disinherited, but can no longer cut themselves off from a call, the echo of which does not cease to resound in inner space, knowing very well that this pure interior is not enough. I have no intention of 'blessing' a kind of secularization; but I do not want to demonize it either. And it is in order to participate in the mystical animation of the growth of humanity that I think it necessary for the churches to be taken out of themselves.[11] If in the eyes of sociologists there is an 'eclipse of the sacred',[12] this could well be in order to allow the mystical experience to happen and to take its expected place. That is why I cannot either rejoice or be satisfied over the emergence of the 'postmodern', which I regard only as a regression to pre-modernity. What we need is a Pascal, and not those emotional devotions which for a moment lead to that 'oceanic sentiment', the term which Romain Rolland used to denote mysticism (letter to Freud, 5 December 1927). Without qualifications or competence, I am more inclined to take Freud's line: he saw in the phenomenon of mysticism not so much the emergence of an original fullness but an incompleteness manifested by division and separation.

If the particular type of mystical witness to which I have referred here is to say to the institutional body, 'You are not everything', nowadays when this type of experience is the secret possession of a large number of people, what we have is a demand for a radical renunciation of the claim to be or represent a perfect society. We cannot identify history and the kingdom. Hannah Arendt saw this point well in connection with the Augustinian theology of history,[13] and it is this that allows and even necessitates a secular approach to history, one which refuses to seek the final point of a definitive society there. One might guess that the mystical irrelevance described above is very important in this period of the mourning of messianisms, as a way of avoiding the impasses of crazy utopias by altering them at the centre, at the 'blind spot'.

And perhaps the silence (sometimes bordering on muteness) which is commonly put somewhere at the heart of mystical experience essentially indicates the impossibility of having an institutional interlocutor. But 'does the silence which speaks in us of an absolute difference need to be socially announced, legislated and ordained by the institutional church to burden our existence'?[14]

> 'If no one had told me that it was love,
> I would have thought that it was a naked sword.'
>
>   (from an ancient Indian poet)

At the Correr Museum in Venice one can see a Tintoretto painting representing a Christ on the cross, exuding a yellowish brightness. Broad-bottomed and chubby angels are hovering round him; dead souls are shamelessly staring at him.

The exile of mysticism is a rejection of this theatre of voyeurism. It establishes in history a silence which is not closed, an echo of the silence which once could be heard over Calvary. The place of mysticism is simply the necessarily sparse expression in writing of this abandonment.

Does not this interminable silence continue at the heart of the real absence that the mystic questions, between the rending of the veil which reveals an empty temple and a stone rolled aside opening an empty tomb, the sole attestation that death is not the last word in a corpse. This abandonment, this stripping, this void, this abandonment in fact represent the glorification of the relationship between God and the world: here is a brightness which does not blind and yet has the greatness of the dawn and the twilight.

Then a figure appears, full of the desire for immediacy and a victim of institutional control: Mary Magdalene. Credited by the Fourth Gospel with all the qualities of an apostle, she has been overshadowed by others. It is a good thing that legend made her a *public* woman. The event which expresses itself in advance through the figure of Mary Magdalene is there in its entirety in her body: and it is not unimportant for its meaning that this is a *woman's* body. Very early on this grey morning, when it is still dark, she is there saying: 'They have taken away my Lord and I do not know where they have laid him.' And she weeps – tears with a salty taste. Her body turns once, twice, so that she no longer knows where she is or where she is looking. Her body is still her body, but it is no longer positioned: it is de-positioned. Her body is a deposition, a witness. He says to her: 'Let me go, do not hold me, I am going to my Father; go to your brothers'. To go to the Father is the same as to go to one's brothers, and that articulates all mystical witness.

> It is time to open a door
> in our resigned silence.
> It is time to live the flesh of time
> in our own flesh.
> See, the waiting is not boundless.
> It is fear which holds us in the night
> and night that holds us in death,
> but not completely, for here and there
> life resists even in the shadows
> and light awaits its hour.

A patience recalls us again to ourselves,
which raises us up and joins us.
Where will the earth take us?
where will our hunger and thirst take us?
We go forward together
these questions engraced in the shadow of our faces;
also for the issues, for that story
which is handed down and which runs:
'they told you, but I tell you'
in which nothing can truly be caught in the trace of habits.

'So that the animal which had been surrounded could find a way out, I flew over the camp of the hunters to disturb their sleep and called out that the way was free' (Jean Sulivan).

Translated by Mortimer Bear

Notes

1. Henri de Lubac, *Corpus mysticum*, Paris [2]1949.
2. Among others, M. D. Chenu, *La théologie au XIIe siècle*, Paris 1957; Jacques le Goff, *Pour une autre Moyen-âge*, Paris 1977.
3. J. Leclercq, 'Les paradoxes de l'économie monastique', *Economie et humanisme* 17, January/February 1945.
4. Ivan Groby, *Saint François d'Assise*, Paris 1957.
5. St Teresa of Avila, *Oeuvres complètes*, Paris 1949, 552.
6. Cf. D de Courcelles, in *Penser la foi – Mélanges offerts à J. Moingt*, Paris 1993, 585–99.
7. D. W. Winnicott, *Playing and Reality*, London 1971; cf. also Richard Kearney, *Poétique du Possible*, Paris 1984.
8. Stanislas Breton, *Du principe*, Paris 1971, 165–70; id., 'Le nécessité de parler doit s'accomoder d'une impossibilité dont le discours comme le corps portent la blessure', in *Deux mystiques de l'excès: J. J. Surin et Maître Eckart*, Paris 1985, 191.
9. Emmanuel Levinas, *L'au delà du verset*, Paris 1982, 134.
10. Michel le Certeau, *La fable mystique*, Paris 1982, 116.
11. It is regrettable that in the recent Universal Catechism, of the eleven uses of the term mystical ten rightly denote the church as 'mystical body'.
12. Cf. Sabino Acquaviva, *L'éclipse du sacré dans la civilisation industrielle*, Paris 1967.
13. Hannah Arendt, *La crise de la culture. Huit exercices de pensée politique*, Paris 1972, 89.
14. Michel de Certeau, *Le christianisme éclaté*, Paris 1974, 26.

Postscript
The Institution and Diversion

Christian Duquoc

The mystical approach to God follows an arduous path: those who commit themselves to this path cannot indulge in sensibility or sentiment. The articles in this issue bear witness to the distinctiveness of such a path: it stands apart from ordinary religion.

The mystical approach is one of persistent will. But there is nothing of voluntarism or perfectionism about it. The will focusses itself unconditionally on the coming of the Other, who is near yet different: it allows itself to be wounded by his presence at the heart of the accepted inability to possess him. This path involves tearing oneself away from a great deal; following it necessarily means discarding the peripheral forms of desire. It requires living in a place where birth to oneself goes along with the coming of the Other. Joy bursts out in this place, but it is always a place of night.

'Remain in hell, but do not despair,' Christ is said to have said to St Sylvanus in a vision. This monk was tormented by a flood of passions which he found great difficulty in controlling; he was afflicted by his sensitivity to the seduction of sin; he was in anguish at discovering the abyss between the ideal of perfection to which he aspired and the mediocrity of his everyday life. Christ told him to remain in this hell, born of the contradiction between the infinity of his desire and the narrowness of his action – but not to despair of his Word. The situation of numerous mystics is described here in the succinct phrase, 'Remain in hell.' Their habitat is the night, and in this night a presence announces itself or a word is spoken which drives off despair.

This saying of Christ to St Sylvanus reminds me of a remark made in quite a different context: a television broadcast on hope. Highly cultured people of different national backgrounds, philosophical and religious, were serenely discussing the topic. Their diagnosis of our society was harsh, their prognoses of its future pessimistic. Neither politics nor the economy nor culture nor even science and technology induced them to optimism. One of them, Michel Serres, ended the discussion with this thought: 'I no longer have any hope, but I keep hoping.'

We are doomed to hell, but in this hell a word can come; it is improbable, it leaves the possibility of hope. In this situation is there not an analogy, albeit a superficial one, with the trial of St Sylvanus? The comparison does not seem to me to be an arbitrary one. Certainly in this broadcast Michel Serres was not concerned with the destiny of the individual; he was thinking of collective history. He noted that our age has given up on utopias, ideologies of progress, religious messianisms, and has taken note of the deterioration in our environment. History no longer has the glorious aura bestowed on it by its movement towards a radiant future. We are caught up in a vicious circle, since all material, scientific and theological progress engenders its opposite. Perhaps it is in this collective night that a word of hope can come – unhoped-for because it is so improbable; hope presupposes actual reasons for tracing out a future full of promise. These reasons are based on what are judged the positive possibilities of the present. For us, according to our thinker, there is nothing of the sort: it seems to us as if the positive elements have been withdrawn. 'Remain in hell, but do not despair.' The mystical path imposed by Christ on St Sylvanus evokes our state to all our contemporaries, now that we have again become clear about the supposed progressive and automatic development of history. We have reaped the bitter fruits of that. It is in this personal and collective failure to see the foundations for hope that a nocturnal invocation can be born. A Swiss poet, Philippe Jacottet, expresses the lure and the desire most beautifully:

> One favour to ask of the distant gods,
> the mute, blind, uninterested gods,
> those runaways:
> that for every tear shed
> by the neighbour, an indestructible grain of wheat
> should germinate in the invisible earth.

The way of the mystics is a way of night.

> Despite the journey we have made, we are at the edge,
> I pass, I am amazed, and I can say no more.

To say more in our situation would be a lie. We have to persevere in this 'prayer which is spoken without the intention of praying and not knowing who might be hearing'.

How do we bear such a night?

What relationship does this path have to the institutional church? The reader will have noted that the articles in this issue all indicate the distance which exists between mystical endurance and institutional interests. Some of the authors strongly emphasize the inevitability of this distance and how beneficial it is. In their view the institutions encourage the discernment of lures which often encumber the mystical path; they preserve the authenticity of the link with God and introduce a law of exteriorization, of solidarity in community. In our dark situation they are the necessary mediation of an ambiguous presence which cannot be grasped. They impose a reality principle on the erring ways of desire that are always possible. Other authors are more polemical, and regret that the institutions, out of a concern to regulate the relationship with God, declare themselves to be absolutely necessary mediations and restrict the extraordinary diversity and wealth of the nocturnal hope and the divine immediacy to the meanness of the observance of an ecclesiastical discipline.

I have noticed, unless I am mistaken, that one aspect of the role of the institution in access to God has been passed over in silence: that of diversion. Not everyone can 'remain in hell' without despairing. Not everyone can live in the dark night without the risk of going mad. People need havens of rest and compassion. It might seem surprising that these have anything to do with diversion, but I think that here we have a major role of the institutional church, a role which is too often forgotten because of our concern for rigour.

The institution is in fact what frees us from having to confront the void or the night, the suffering of profound desire, the intolerable pressure of a burning presence. The institution smoothes over the breaks. In a television broadcast a hermit remarked: 'Almost all people live on the periphery of their being. The tragedy is not death, but that people can die without having the least idea of the infinite riches they have within themselves.'

I have asked myself whether this remark did not lack compassion. Gaining access to these riches calls for a way so rough and painful that the majority of people avoid it; they would fall by the wayside out of weariness, anxiety or madness. Rightly, they are offered a different way: the institutional church offers an alternative more suited to the weakness and mediocrity of the average person, diverting him or her from the void that they would have to face and in which they would be swallowed up.

How can we bear the night? Tolerate our lack of knowledge? Undergo the recurrent suffering and manifold evil? Bear a searing presence? Only by turning away to something less real. Pascal speaks of diversion. There is a well-known sentence from a long passage which in my view hides its depth: 'I have discovered that the unhappiness of human beings comes just one thing: not knowing how to remain quietly in a room. If people cannot remain in a room, it is because they are assailed by boredom and anxiety and plain madness roves there.'

'The king is surrounded by people intent only on diverting the king, and preventing him from thinking of himself. For he is unhappy; every king is, if he thinks . . . ' 'The philosophers who think that the world is crazy to spend the day chasing a hare that no one would have wanted to spend money on know very little about our nature. The hare would not protect us from the sight of death and misery, but the hunt which diverts us does.'

Can one apply such vitriolic views to the institutional church without impertinence? Certainly, but on one condition, that the diversion is a means necessary for the equilibrium of believers; that those who preside over it know its limits and do not go beyond them. In this perspective, the institutional church performs three functions: it gathers a symbolic assembly; it defines a discipline; and it provides an object for aggression.

A symbolic assembly: as Jesus said to the Samaritan woman, God is not worshipped on Gerizim or in Jerusalem, but in Spirit and in truth. The institution does not put this saying of Jesus in question, but it cannot be content with it if it wants to gather a people. So it has fixed places and times when men and women come together, so that crowds symbolically become people, by actions which they perform together: the liturgy in its different forms of celebration, pilgrimages to the tombs of saints or places of appearances. These activities involve the people: they allow them to live out the presence of the God who is beyond our grasp in festivities and brotherhood and sisterhood. So the institution imitates the kingdom while knowing and preaching that the kingdom is elsewhere. John Paul II has well understood this need for religious festivity. He gathers crowds, reassures them with strong words, they applaud him and do as they please. He has diverted them in an institutional way. The only obstacle is the repetition of the same game, which tends to take the edge off it.

The debate on popular religions which keeps cropping up within the church is rooted in this necessity: the institutions are works of compassion, since no one knows where the Spirit comes from or where it goes. This wandering is too hard to bear, and the institutions mark out a way for it. However, one can hope that the church authorities are aware of this wandering: their task is to be open to the burning presence by effacing themselves little by little as mediators and by teaching.

To define a discipline: 'Love, and do what you want' said St Augustine. No one would dream to put in question so elevated and apparently liberating a principle. However, the institution which brings crowds together to make them a people cannot be content with it. For the weak and those who are not yet enlightened it has to fix more precise points of reference to sustain co-existence, make prohibitions which hinder the opening up of the human community or whose absence would lead to the disintegration of the structure of the personality. In short, an institution is a place in which an ethic is imposed in the senses that it encourages laudable customs and develops a morality; in the sense that it orientates itself on the irreplaceable subjective conscience. Its rules and imperatives provide a diversion from the anguish of creation and responsibility: they give freedom from the void over which the Augustinian principle 'Love and do what you want' hovers. But if one wants the diversion to be educational, and if one denies that it hides access to God, it must be indwelt by a concern on the part of the authorities to put at a distance the moral conscience and objectivity of institutional truth. Otherwise the teacher becomes a tyrant and the concern to serve a concern for power, and in providing distraction from the void, diversion would be making slaves.

To provide an object for aggression: Jacob and Job fought against God, and God proved them right. However, this fight is bold and perilous, since God is ineffable and beyond our grasp. Koheleth says that we don't know what we are doing. These struggles have also been handed down to us in lofty poetic images. The claims and pretensions of the institutional church often seem banale and everyday; despite the witness that it bears to Christ it adopts questionable ways. In so doing it opens up an endless debate on what it should say, practise and promise. It provides an object for aggression. Eugen Drewermann relates a conversation he had with a pilot. At the end of their dialogue, the pilot said to him: 'I left the church years ago . . . The priest always seemed to me like a prison warder. For him, the least question was already a blasphemy.'

This story of Drewermann's reminds me of an anecdote which explains the aggression that the institution can arouse. A bishop now dead, it is said, had been elevated to the cardinalate. Returning from Rome where this honour had been conferred on him, he said as he got out of the town in his home city, 'All my desires have been fulfilled.' This supreme diversion, having attained the highest honours (the cardinalate is to faith what the French Academy is to literary creation), had extinguished the question: how do we face the night of access to God without going mad? There remained the institution, its discipline and its trappings: raising any question here seemed tasteless. One can understand how the priest of whom Drewermann spoke had provoked the aggression of the pilot. He had perverted his role: he had diverted to the point of suppressing the gap between the institution and the God to whom he had to bear witness. In doing this the institution allows God to live in freedom. The mediocrity of church government as compared with the loftiness of its ideals encourages the regulation of aggression in religious matters. That is not without benefits for faith.

However, far be it from me to confine the church to one of its institutional roles, diversion, in other words to allow those who cannot bear the ultimate question to survive in faith or to follow without becoming unbalanced the arduous path of immediate access to God. Diversion cannot be a substitute for the way itself: if the institution itself becomes a way, it ceases to be a work of compassion: it imprisons, and drives to despair. Better then to follow Christ's advice to St Sylvanus: 'remain in hell and do not despair'.

Translated by John Bowden

Demands of the Indigenous Peoples

Never before has it been so urgent a task to establish new relations between peoples and employ all our creativity to devise mechanisms that will make the international community realize the need for real respect for human rights and integral development without discrimination as the twin foundations for a new society.

The new millennium which is approaching is also a critical and painful situation for the most vulnerable and defenceless sectors of humanity. They are reacting strongly with demands that create a growing emergency leading to social and political upheavals in a number of countries. These situations have provoked widespread discussion and debate not only within the countries affected, but also in the main international forums.

A constant element in all these discussions is a series of demands put forward by the indigenous peoples on numerous occasions within their own countries. There are also joint resolutions resulting from debate and reflection of different peoples presented at various times in different international forums for consideration by the international community.

We indigenous peoples demand that the international forums include on their agendas discussions on the issue of the self-determination of indigenous peoples, and as a result issue guidelines on its meaning and scope to be observed by national governments, the big financial institutions such as the World Bank and the Inter-American Development Bank, and by the various non-governmental organizations.

In this process the indigenous peoples have obtained important gains in the international community, notably participation as a single group at the Rio Environment Summit and the Vienna Summit on Human Rights, the holding of the First Summit Meeting of Indigenous Peoples in Chimaltenango, Guatemala, and the Second Summit in Oaxtepec, Mexico, among others.

Another demand has been granted with the approval by the United

Nations of the Preparatory Year for the International Decade of Indigenous Peoples. Some countries have also begun to sign Convention 169 of the International Labour Organization, which creates new labour relations for indigenous peoples.

This indigenous participation in international debate did not develop spontaneously, but was a gradual product of the International Year of Indigenous Peoples. The Year also initiated the request of the United Nations to declare a decade to consolidate the formal creation of spaces for debate and discussion on issues concerning indigenous peoples and Original World Peoples. In the past these issues have not received serious treatment based on respect and equality, and more often than not have not even been given adequate space for discussion. The approval of the International Decade, to begin on 1 December 1994, and its preparatory year, gives the opportunity to face the great issues on our agenda as a large number of demands are formally presented.

In this context I have called on my indigenous brothers and sisters of the whole world to join the Indigenous Initiative for Peace, whose first mission has been completed in Chiapas. In addition to this, however, it is necessary to establish the right of the indigenous community to play a direct, active and permanent role in debate and discussion on the great issues affecting every community and the international community in general. In this connection, the consolidation of the Indigenous Initiative for Peace as a permanent forum provides a space in which the indigenous themselves can take part in the recording and investigation of any human rights abuses, especially those against indigenous peoples.

At the same time we entertain the hope that one day the Indigenous Initiative for Peace may be recognized as a specialized organ of the United Nations. While the Initiative will not be able to solve all problems, it will have the right to be heard in all international institutions, in the European Union and other major international blocs and may form a space for pooling analyses of development co-operation and political relations between the European states and Third World countries.

Rigoberta Menchú
1992 Nobel Peace Prize Winner

Translated by Francis McDonagh

The editors of the Special Column are Norbert Greinacher and Bas van Iersel. The content of the Special Column does not necessarily reflect the views of the Editorial Board of Concilium.

Contributors

YVES CATTIN is Associate Professor of Philosophy in the Philosophy Department of the Blaise Pascal University of Clermont-Ferrand, France. In addition to numerous articles on philosophy he has written two books: *La preuve de Dieu*, Paris 1987; *Court traité de l'existence chrétienne*, Paris 1992.

Address: Saignes, 63710 St Nectaire, France.

CARLO CAROZZO was born in 1940 and studied philosophy and pedagogics; married, he has been editor of the Genoan journal *Il Gallo* since 1960. He has collected and edited the writings of Katy Canavero, the stories and reflections of a woman who suffered for fifteen years from cancer (*Una fede difficile*, Turin 1989) and with her wrote *Alla tavola dei peccatore* (1969) and a study on Job; other books include *L'amore e il potere – Amos e Osea* (1971). With friends from *Il Gallo* he has worked on three small volumes: *Riscorire la preghiera* (1984), *Vivere il quotidiano* (1988) and *Credo la vita eterna* (1989).

Address: Il Gallo, Casella Postale 1242, 16100 Genoa, Italy.

SEBASTIAN KAPPEN was born in Kerela, India, in 1924, became a Jesuit in 1944 and gained a doctorate in theology at Gregorianum, Rome, in 1961. For over thirty years he was actively engaged in dialogue with Marxism, theological reflection on socio-cultural issues and guidance of social action groups. Besides numerous articles in theological journals he published the books: *Jesus and Freedom* (1977), *Marxian Atheism* (1983), *Jesus and Cultural Revolution – An Asian Perspective* (1984); *The Future of Socialism, and the Socialism of the Future* (1992) and *Tradition, Modernity and Counterculture* (1994). This article for *Concilium* was completed just two days before he died, on 1 December 1993 at Bangalore.

SEBASTIAN PAINADATH was born in Kerela, India in 1942. He became a Jesuit in 1966 and gained a doctorate in theology at Tübingen in 1978. In 1987 he founded Sameeksha, Centre for Indian Spirituality, at Kalady,

India, where he offers regular courses in Indian Christian Spirituality and Interreligious Dialogue. He teaches Theology of Religions at the Faculties in Pune and Delhi, and every year conducts spirituality seminars in Germany. His publications include *Dynamics of Prayer*, Bangalore 1980, and *Jesu Vyaktiyum Saktiyum* (Towards an Indian Christology), Kottayam 1992.

Address: Sameeksha, Kalady, 683574, India.

WILLIGIS JÄGER was born in 1925. He is a Benedictine of Münsterschwarzach Abbey. He studied philosophy and theology, was ordained and then spent a long period in a Japanese Zen Centre. He is a Zen Master of the San Bo Kyodan School and head of a Meditation Centre in Würzburg. His books, which have appeared in a number of languages, include *The Way to Contemplation*, New York 1987.

JEAN-CLAUDE SAGNE, OP, was born in 1936 in Tours, France. He studied theology at the Dominican house at Arbresle and was ordained priest in 1963. Qualified in theology and religious psychology, he teaches social psychology at the University of Lyons II. His publications include: *Tes péchés ont été pardonnés*, Paris 1977; *Traité de théologie spirituelle*, Paris 1992.

Address: 2 Place Gaileton, 69002 Lyon, France.

VICTOR CODINA was born in Barcelona in 1931, and joined the Jesuits in 1948. After studying philosophy and theology in Barcelona, Innsbruck and Rome, he was for twenty years professor of systematic theology at the San Cugat Theology Faculty in Barcelona. Since 1982 he has lived in Bolivia, where he worked for a time at the ISET Theological Institute in Cochabama. He currently works on education programmes for lay people and grass-roots groups. His recent publications include *De la modernidad a la solidaridad* (Lima 1984); *Para comprender la eclesiología desde América Latina* (Estella 1990); *Teología simbólica de la tierra* (Bogotá 1993).

GUSTAVO GUTIÉRREZ was born in Lima, Peru, in 1928, and after studying medicine and literature in Peru, studied psychology and philosophy at Louvain and took a doctorate in theology in Lyon. He has been principal professor at the Pontifical Catholic University of Peru since 1960. He is world famous as one of the founders of the theology of liberation, notably through his book *A Theology of Liberation* (1971, new ed. 1988). He has written on spirituality especially in *The Power of the Poor in History* (1983), *We Drink from Our Own Wells* (1984) and *On Job. God-Talk and the Suffering of the Innocent* (1987).

His contribution to the theology of liberation has brought him honorary doctorates from ten universities in five countries, and in 1993 he was awarded the Legion of Honour by the French government for his 'tireless work for human dignity and life, and against oppression, in Latin America and the Third World'.

GÉRARD ROLLAND was born in Perigueux in 1941 and is a priest in the diocese of Versailles. He was ordained in 1968 after five years pastoral work in the industrial valley of the Seine, and then taught at the school of faith and ministry at Fribourg, Switzerland until 1977. From 1981 until 1989 he was Catholic director of the Ecumenical Workshop of Theology in Geneva and from 1987 to 1993 almoner of the university world in Geneva, where in parallel he became Secretary General of the International Catholic Centre in Geneva. He is now auxiliary priest in a country area of Geneva.

Address: 30 rue de Candolle, 1205 Geneva, Switzerland.

Members of the Advisory Committee for Spirituality

Yearbook/Jahrbuch Vol 2/1994 of the European Society of Women in Theological Research

Ecofeminism and Theology
Mary Grey and Elizabeth Green (eds.)

CONTENTS

FORUM: on Ecofeminism and the Ecological Crisis

FRAUENTRADITIONEN:

Publishing Date: August 1994   ISBN: 90 390 0204 5
Paperback   approx. 160pp   approx. £14.00 (members ESWTR 10% discount)

**Order: Kok Pharos Publishing House, P O Box 5016
8260 GA Kampen, The Netherlands**

Concilium Subscription Information - outside North America

Individual Annual Subscription (six issues): £30.00

Institution Annual Subscription (six issues): £40.00

Airmail subscriptions: add £10.00

Individual issues: £8.95 each

New subscribers please return this form:
for a two-year subscription, double the appropriate rate

(for individuals) £30.00 (1/2 years) . . . .

(for institutions) £40.00 (1/2 years) . . . .

Airmail postage
outside Europe +£10.00 (1/2 years) . . . .

Total . . . .

I wish to subscribe for one/two years as an individual/institution
(delete as appropriate)

Name/Institution . . . .

Address . . . .

. . . .

. . . .

I enclose a cheque for . . . . payable to SCM Press Ltd

Please charge my Access/Visa/Mastercard no. . . . .

Signature . . . . .Expiry Date . . . .

Please return this form to:
SCM PRESS LTD 26-30 Tottenham Road, London N1 4BZ